The Crack

Michael Munro
Illustrated by Bob Dewar

BIRLINN

New edition first published in Great Britain in 2002 by
Birlinn Ltd
West Newington House
10 Newington Road
Edinburgh EH9 1QS

www.birlinn.co.uk

Reprinted 2005, 2007
Reprinted with revisions 2013

ISBN: 978 1 78027 182 8

British Library Cataloguing in Publication Data

A catalogue record for this book is available from the British Library.

Typeset by Palimpsest Book Production Limited,
Falkirk, Stirlingshire
Printed and bound by
Grafica Veneta
www.graficaveneta.com

Contents

Introduction

THIS IS a collection of Glasgow humour, including anecdotes, stories, and jokes. For many of these, the humour turns on the Glaswegian use of language and in most cases on what might be identified as a Glaswegian way of looking at things. I intend to go no further in trying to pin down exactly what it is that constitutes Glasgow humour; once you start analysing comedy, not only do you miss the point but it's suddenly not funny any more.

Humour is important in Glasgow life. A look at the history of popular entertainment in the city shows that Glasgow has always enjoyed a good laugh and the home-grown variety best of all. Professional comedians often shared the background of their audiences, having sprung from working-class tenements and retaining intimate knowledge of all the drawbacks of tenement life (overcrowding, damp, insanitary conditions) as well as the points to be celebrated (neighbourliness, the shared humour in the face of adversity, the stairheid gossip) that fostered a sense of community. A long line of Glasgow comedians came out of this home background, their wit further honed by the working environment of various of the city's major industries. Any list must include: Tommy Lorne, Tommy Morgan (a native of Bridgeton who worked in a chocolate factory before getting into a concert party in the army), Dave Willis (a New City Road butcher's son who served an engineering apprenticeship), Alex Finlay, Jack Anthony, Clarke and Murray (known as 'Mr and Mrs Glasgow'), Chic Murray (like his admirer Billy Connolly, a one-time shipyard worker), and Lex McLean (known as 'Sexy Lexie', not for arousing desire but because his material could be as blue as his nose), to name but millions.

Some of these stage acts, like Rikki Fulton and Jack Milroy's 'Francie and Josie' and Stanley Baxter, made a successful transition to the very much wider audience of television, establishing a line of Glasgow humour on TV which extends through *Rab C. Nesbitt, Chewin' the Fat, Still Game, Burnistoun* and *Limmy's Show*.

Outwith performance, perhaps the funniest and best-loved exponent of Glaswegian humour is the cartoonist William 'Bud' Neill. His individual cartoons appeared in the *Evening Times* from the 1940s on, including as his principal stock characters two buxom wifies deliberating fearlessly and candidly on everything from their latest aches and pains to *Julius Caesar*: 'It's aboot a lot o' blokes in nightgoons stabbin' some old joker wi' a crew cut, and the patter's wicked.' Neill is probably most affectionately remembered for his serial strip 'Lobey Dosser', the horse opera with a Glasgow accent, commemorated by a statue in the city's West End of the hero alongside his arch enemy Rank Bajin, both borne by Lobey's two-legged horse El Fideldo.

Neill was also responsible for various gems of vernacular verse, some of which have achieved the true fame of being quotable by lots of people who couldn't name the poet. Best known of these must be 'Perishin' Poem':

> Winter's came,
> The snow has fell,
> Wee Josie's nosis frozis well,
> Wee Josie's frozen nosis skintit,
> Winter's diabolic, intit?

Bud Neill died in 1970 having single-handedly set in motion a wave of Glasgow cartoon humour on which have surfed, in their own individual styles, such artists as Willie Gall, Malky McCormick, and (to wilder shores than ever) the contributors to the comic periodical *Electric Soup*.

No look at Glasgow humour could leave out Billy Connolly. I first became aware of him in the early 1970s, just before he became really hot property, when he was touring his act of music and comedy around the folk clubs, pubs, social clubs, and student unions of Scotland. His sketches and long routines like 'The Crucifixion' or 'Harry Campbell and the Heavies', much interrupted by enormously digressive adlibs and crushing putdowns of hecklers, paraded a kind of comedy contemporary audiences had never seen on stage before and hadn't realised until then how much we needed. Connolly's gifts of observation and storytelling, and instinct for pinpointing mercilessly the ludicrous in the everyday, combined with the worldly-but-amused delivery of a Glasgow patter-merchant *par excellence*, constituted a revelation that inspired countless amateur imitators.

In a way this was closing the circle, as Connolly's inspiration, like that of many of his predecessors, was the natural, spontaneous, everyday wit of his fellow citizens. This is what this book, rather than the routines of the professionals, is chiefly about. Much of the material in these pages consists of jokes and stories that Glaswegians recount to amuse themselves and others, not well-rehearsed stand-up acts. It is well known that the true stories and events are often the funniest, and I would like to point out that every story contained herein is absolutely true (except for the made-up ones). Some of the stories fall into the category often known as urban myths. I like to call them 'palamines', because the teller usually describes the events related as happening to 'a pal of mine'. Such tales may well have begun with a kernel of actuality but by the time they have been in circulation for a while the 'Chinese whispers' effect comes into play and they can part company with the real events. What they gain is the elaboration and embroidery of several active imaginations – not so much economical with the truth as spendthrift with the creativity – until the final version is an example of a kind of folk-art, far superior to the mundane original.

Readers should note that I do not claim that all of the material in this collection is new; far from it. Many of these jokes and stories have been around for generations.

To anyone who encounters something he has heard before I would say only this: there is no such thing as a new joke. Humour is endlessly recyclable and, while many instances of it are topical (and often all the more funny for that), anything too closely tied to a particular time or event will not last. Therefore, if it is said that some of these stories have a beard on them it is because they capture something unchanging about what makes Glaswegians laugh.

Collecting the material, while usually fun in itself, was not always easy. People when put on the spot and asked to come out with some funnies often experience a mental block and the Saturday night life-and-soul can suddenly seem bereft of inspiration. Because of this I am even more conscious of the debt I owe to those who contributed material (some of whom didn't know they were doing it) and my particular thanks go to: Michael Coyle, Neil Davies, Tom Docherty, Lorna Gilmour, Martin Gray, Graham Hamilton, Willie Hanlon, Heather Hunt, David Liston, Terry McCann, Ranald MacColl, Boyd McNicol, Edwin Moor, Alice Munro, Daniel M. Munro, Tom Neilson, Pat Phillips, Dave Pretswell, Douglas Reid, Billy Ross, Tom Shearer, Padam Singh, Alan Torrance, Archie White, Hamish Wilson and Kenneth Wright.

Michael Munro
Glasgow, 2013

The Work

A WORKPLACE tends to be a fertile source of humour. Even though the appreciation of much of this will depend on knowledge of the characters involved, it is a poor trade or profession that never yields a funny story or two. Indeed, sometimes being able to laugh at it is all that makes employment (or unemployment) tolerable at all. It is always a joy to find yourself working alongside a real patter-merchant (and I have been lucky enough to rub shoulders with a few) whose stories, and it doesn't matter if they're true or not as long as they're funny, help keep everyone going.

A MANAGER was once explaining to his secretary that her old electric typewriter was about to be replaced with a state-of-the-art PC with an all-powerful word-processing software package. He was at pains to convince her that this equipment upgrade would be of great benefit to all, not least to the secretary herself, who could now venture forth onto the open seas of desktop publishing. The girl was unimpressed. Being of a suspicious and conservative nature, she anticipated another sly way of giving her even more work to do for the same pittance she already received. Her problem was that, try as she might, she could see no reasonable way of objecting to what her boss was telling her.

By now he was extolling the virtues of the printer that was part of the package, emphasising its speed and ability to produce fairly sophisticated documents with ease. There was only one drawback compared to her existing typewriter, which was that the printer could be pretty noisy in operation. The manufacturers had anticipated this problem, however, and one of the accessories that came as standard was a specially-designed noise-reducing acoustic hood. At this point the secretary, triumphantly seizing on something she thought she could legitimately object to, touched her fingertips to her expensively-styled hair and pronounced:

'Acoustic hood? No way am Ah wearing wan a thame!'

EVEN IN times of relatively low unemployment there are those to whom the idea of working for a living is anathema. Wee Tam was famous both for his aversion to honest toil and his energy in avoiding it. Two of his acquaintances were discussing him one day.

'Ye should've seen Wee Tam at the Jobcentre the day . . . he was gaun pure mental.'

'Mental, wis he?'

'Aye, they were tryin tae get wan a thae jackets on him.'

'Whit – a straitjacket?'

'Naw, a donkey jacket.'

IN A city-centre office a group of secretaries and office juniors discovered that they had a common enthusiasm for the music of Kylie. It so happened that the object of their admiration was coming to Glasgow for a performance in a few months' time. The ladies decided to start saving a regular certain amount from their pay so as to be able to afford not only the concert tickets but a good night afterwards with a meal and a few drinks. The arrangement worked very smoothly; the regular deductions from their take-home pay were modest enough and they hardly missed the money at all. On the big night itself a thoroughly splendid time was enjoyed by all concerned.

Deciding that this was a painless way to fund further nights out, the ladies agreed to keep their savings club going and made it a permanent feature of their working life. There was no doubt about it that the name they had used was too good to change and it is known to this day as the Kylie Menodge.

I WAS told the following tale by the individual involved. A tradesman is awakened by his alarm clock one morning.

He reaches out one hand, his only movement, to switch the thing off, conscious that he has a sore head. He lies there trying to compose himself before summoning the effort to get up. He knows that he doesn't have a great deal of time before he must catch his lift to work. He becomes conscious that something is not quite as normal, but can't fix on what it is. Opening his eyes and looking down at his feet he sees that they are enclosed in his working boots. He is not in his bed but on it. Not only is he still wearing yesterday's clothes but his parka is still on and the hood is tied tightly about his head. It all comes back to him now: he went for a pint with his mates straight from work. One pint led to another, and . . . after that it became hazy. His nose detects a smell not normally associated with lying in bed. Looking just below his chin he spots, resting on his chest, what he easily identifies as a pie supper, still in its wrappings, with only a couple of chips missing. He lifts it off and puts it aside, then staggers to the bathroom. He completes his toilet, including splashing water on his face, without so much as taking down his parka hood and heads out into the street.

I am lost in admiration, then a thought occurs to me:

'I bet that pie supper didn't smell too pleasant when you came home that day.'

'Don't be daft. Ah had that fur ma breakfast. Ah didny want tae miss ma lift!'

HAVING LOST his job, a man turns up at his benefit office to register as unemployed. He goes through all the form-filling and other routines and is told that a giro will be sent out to him. It duly arrives and he goes to his local post office to cash it. To his unutterable chagrin they refuse to carry out the transaction as they have no record of him having nominated that particular post office as his local one when he signed on. He goes back to the benefit office and it is discovered that he neglected to nominate any post office at all. Someone at the DSS had realised this and decided to nominate one for him. Seeing that his address was in Rutherglen Road the well-intentioned functionary had assumed that this was in Rutherglen and it was to a post office in that fair burgh that his details had been sent. Apologies were duly made. Things would be put right for next time but there was nothing for it but that he would have to go to Ru'glen to cash his first giro.

The claimant was unimpressed by this misguided attempt to be helpful. His only comment was to thank his luck (or something that sounded like that) that he didn't live in London Road.

THIS ONE goes all the way back to World War I. Earl Haig was making a tour of inspection at the Western Front when he came across a section of the line that was currently held by the HLI. The Highland Light Infantry (not the Hairy-Legged Irishmen as some wags would have it) was based at Maryhill Barracks and had a large proportion of Glaswegians in its ranks. It was to one of these, a young private who struck the Earl as an intelligent-looking soldier, that the brass hat addressed a standard conversational enquiry.

'Well, my man,' he said, 'and where did you start the war?'

The soldier paled but managed to stammer out,

'It wisny me, sir. Swear tae Goad it wisny!'

LIFE CAN be harsh in the building trade; you've got to be able to take the rough with the smooth, give as good as you get in the hard knocks' stakes. Individuals can make over-hasty judgments about one another but trade-wide reputations are seldom wrong. There was a site foreman who was known to all who worked with him as The Pig. This was not because of his physical appearance (although by all accounts he was no honey) but down to his unreasonable behaviour. He was unmoved by abuse, and when one worker whom he had occasion to sack tried to get

revenge by revealing that everybody hated him and called him The Pig, the gaffer merely observed in a deadpan voice:

'I'm deeply hurt; on your way.'

One day The Pig fell from a scaffolded building. Apparently it was a bona fide accident but, either way, the victim was left with two broken arms. One of the workers accompanied the boss to hospital and was told that he would be kept in overnight to be discharged with both arms in plaster the next day. Accordingly, a few of them from the site turned up to meet him and insisted on taking him for a pint to show there were no hard feelings. As he couldn't move either arm at all the lads took turns at holding his pint tumbler up to his mouth for him. And they certainly made sure he had plenty of pints. What with the beer, the debilitating effects of his experiences, and the effects of his painkillers, The Pig soon became distinctly woozy and his companions insisted on taking him home. They hadn't gone far along the street when The Pig let them know he was in pressing need of a urination; the thing was, one of them would have to give him a hand. This was the cue they had been waiting for. Snow off a dyke wasn't in it as they all immediately disappeared.

WORKING AWAY from home can have its advantages, both for those doing the working and those left back at the ranch. Sometimes distance does not make the heart grow fonder, as the following poignant vignette illustrates. There was a Glasgow roustabout called Frankie who was working away on an oil rig somewhere in the wild wastes of the North Sea. He had already spent Christmas offshore and when Hogmanay came around he had to let his wife back in Springburn know that he wasn't going to be coming home for the festivities. Out of the blue, one of his mates told him that he'd changed his mind about going ashore that evening on the last available helicopter.

If Frankie wanted it, the seat was his. It was a last-minute affair and Frankie just had time to get the boss's agreement on the exchange, pack a bag and head off without phoning home.

As they lifted off, the weather, already grim, began to worsen until it wasn't a fit night for man, beast nor roustabout. The pilot resolved to battle on. It was a rough flight for all the passengers and Frankie wasn't the only one to think, more than once, that his last minute had come as the aircraft was buffeted by winds and seemed destined to end up in the water.

When they finally landed they were greeted by driving snow as they struggled to the relative shelter of the terminal. Frankie joined the queue of people waiting to use the phone, grateful to have made it this far, wondering how he was going to get from here to Glasgow in these conditions. What the hell, he thought, it might be a real struggle he was facing yet but he would make it! He got through to his home number and his wife answered after quite a few rings. Her voice sounded a bit cross.

'Hello, hen!' cried the triumphant Frankie, 'Guess what? Ah'm gauny be hame for the New Year after aw! You wouldny believe the journey Ah've hud.'

His wife cut him off.

'Aye, very good. But could ye no ring back? Ah'm in the middle of watchin I. M. Jolly.'

IN ONE particular place of work there was a manager known to all employees as Subway; the reason being that he came round every five minutes. I also heard tell of a worker in a shipyard who was nicknamed The Destroyer, not because he was particularly unskilful, but because he was always looking for a sub.

A FRIEND of mine who is a Careers Officer told me about one of his first days at work after starting this new job. He was sent to a Glasgow school to give the fourth year a talk on career options. He had been warned that the school in question was on the rough side and he might expect to get a certain amount of teasing from the pupils. He overcame any trepidation and was pleased to find that they listened to him attentively enough. After his talk, he asked if anyone knew for certain what they wanted to be after leaving school and was gratified when a boy immediately thrust up his hand.

'So what is it you want to be?'

'Sir! A muff-diver!'

THERE CAN be few more thankless jobs of work than being a rent-collector in a poor area. The story is told of such a person in the old Gorbals who had chapped on every door in a close and had none of them opened to him. To add insult to injury, when he emerged from the closemouth a policeman, summoned by a jocular neighbour, lifted him for begging.

IT CAN be a trauma when large-scale work has to be done on your house, and you can fall prey, as you survey a daily scene of noise and dust, to doubts as to whether you will ever really get back to normal. One particular Bearsden matron, a widow, was finally prevailed upon by her son to have her house rewired before the pre-war wiring caused a fire. She had had no real grasp of the amount of destruction involved: carpets and floorboards lifted, sockets pulled out and new ones dug in, entire walls 'raggled' to expose the cables that were to be ripped out. The electrician himself was an understanding soul and assured her of the pains he would take to minimise the damage. He proved to be a man of his word and this consoled her, but he was assisted by The Apprentice From Hell.

This was a lumpish youth with his hair shaved into the wood, rings in ears and nose, lurid tattoos on his heavily-muscled arms and an inability to concentrate on his task unless his ghetto-blaster was belting out some death-thrash-metal at maximum decibels. He added to the necessary mess by leaving chip-papers and half-empty soft-drink cans lying around and throwing down his tools without concern for varnished floorboards or glossed skirting. The lady of the house was terrified of this creature and while she generally managed to avoid meeting him face to face, the noise of his moving around the house was inescapable. One afternoon when the workers were busy upstairs she decided a restorative G & T would be in order and sat down in the remains of her living room to enjoy it. Just as she began to feel a gentle relaxation stealing over her a louder than usual impact sounded above her head. She looked up to see a size-eleven Doc Marten boot violently materialise through her ceiling in a shower of plaster and obscene oaths. It was the final straw; she collapsed in tears. A few moments later, The Apprentice From Hell appeared, dispatched by his gaffer to see what the damage was. His craggy heart was softened by the sight of an old lady weeping and he bent to put a consoling arm across her frail shoulders.

'Whit's the matter, hen?' he enquired solicitously, 'Is it yer man?'

A BUSINESSMAN was passing through Central Station on his way to an important meeting. It occurred to him that a view of a *Financial Times* would supply him with a piece of information that he felt was crucial to his all-round grasp of the matter that was uppermost on the agenda. Assuming that in such a business-friendly city as Glasgow there would be copies readily available, he approached the station news-stand and, failing to spot the *FT* on the counter, asked the young lady attendant for a copy.

'Sorry, mister,' she shrugged. 'We only get the wan an it's selt.'

IT WAS the last working day before Christmas. Four colleagues decided on a lunchtime pint and made for a venue where they knew they could get a reasonable pub meal. The place was packed with office workers on the same mission, but they spotted two tables for four and claimed one of them. The table was set out as usual with place-mats and cutlery, but seasonally enough a Christmas cracker was also laid out at each setting. Assuming that this was the pub's contribution to the Yuletide spirit, they exuberantly pulled the four crackers, donned the party hats that emerged therefrom and told each other the jokes. At this juncture a waitress appeared.

'Are yous wi the party a eight?' she enquired.

On being answered in the negative, she scolded:

'Well, that's their crackers yeez've went an pullt!'

THEN THERE was the office department whose manager was retiring. He had been the type of boss who is over-full of himself, and when a whip-round was collected to buy him a farewell gift one wag proposed spending the money on an inflatable woman, on the premise that one big balloon deserves another.

One of the Glaswegian seamen my grandfather sailed with was, for some reason, known to all and sundry as Haddieheid, and was accounted by my grandfather 'the best fireman on the Clyde'. The fact that this man was famous throughout the nautical world was shown by the following anecdote.

During the war Haddieheid was serving aboard a vessel in the Atlantic. To the crew's horror, a German U-boat surfaced nearby and began to observe them. The U-boat commander asked his lieutenant to scan the merchant ship with his binoculars to see if he could identify it. The lieutenant was quickly able to do so, but said there was one thing puzzling him. The captain asked what that was, and his officer replied:

'Well, I'm just wonderin who that is on the bridge staunin next tae Haddieheid.'

The captain seized his loud-hailer and called across:
'Hello, Haddieheid!'
He then turned to his officers and let them know:
'We'll no sink this yin, lads. Haddieheid's aboard!'

WILLIE MCILVANNEY tells the story of going to look round a mortuary in the course of his research for his Laidlaw novels. The attendant, no doubt of necessity, had the gallows humour of Glasgow off to a T. When he took the opportunity to show the author the corpse of a person who had been badly burnt in a fire, his comment was:
'The faimly's wantin hauf price at the cremmy!'

SOME OF the kids applying for jobs today lack a grasp of the niceties involved in trying to impress a potential employer. I came across the tale of one such applicant who, with touchingly naive honesty, when confronted with a blank space on her application form where hobbies were to be entered, wrote:
'Sitting on my bum cheeks doing nothing.'
Needless to say, she failed to win the job, but a bright future awaits her in some other field . . . like stand-up comedy.

A POST office worker in a Glasgow sorting office was touched by a handwritten note he happened upon in a batch of mail. It was scrawled in an unsteady hand on a sheet torn from a cheap writing pad, and was addressed to God. It was a plea from a father of four to the Almighty for £50 to buy the children a Christmas present. The writer had tried everything, he said, and this was his last hope.
A whip-round was quickly organised, and despite the short notice, £45 was collected and sent to the address on the letter in time for Christmas. A few days later another leaf from the same pad turned up and in the same hand was written a letter of thanks to God. There was a PS which read thus:

'By the way, it was a fiver short. I blame these thieving bastards in the post office.'

A JOINER from out of town was working in a very run-down scheme on the outskirts of Glasgow. He had been told that anybody with any sense or get-up-and-go had got up and gone somewhere else, leaving only the shift-less and the stupid to inhabit the area. While he was working in one particular house, he fell into conversation with the occupant, who seemed pleasant enough.

'I've heard some stories about this place,' the joiner said.

'Oh aye,' said the other man. 'What like?'

'Well, a mate of mine told me that every second house here has got a total idiot in it.'

'Is that so? The guy next door tae me's awright.'

AND NOW a tale from the shipyards. A man who drove a 'cran' at one of the major yards was reminiscing about the old days and explaining how he would be given the signal to start lifting or lowering a load by the foreman giving a loud blast on a whistle. He remembered the day when a startling innovation was introduced: walkie-talkies, which now allowed the foreman and crane driver to speak to each other directly. He never forgot the first time these were used. The foreman used the radio to ask him if he was ready, and when the driver replied that he was, the foreman nearly burst his eardrums by blowing the whistle into the walkie-talkie.

TWO LADIES having a friendly cup of coffee got around to talking about tradesmen.

'Ye wouldny have the name of a good plumber, would ye?' asked one, 'Every wan Ah get tae come oot tae the hoose is a no-user. Disny fix anythin right and charges ye a fortune.'

'Tell me aboot it!' said the other. 'We've had that many

cowboys in oor hoose we should be flyin the Lone Star of Texas!'

AN ENGLISH sales rep for a well-known multinational company was obliged to attend a marketing conference in one of Glasgow's finest hotels.

As the hotel was extremely busy, the rep was told he would have to share a room with another employee, a man he didn't know, but as he was well used to the ups and downs of a life on the road, this didn't concern him greatly and he was sure that when they met they would get on like a house on fire.

The hospitality of the hosting team was, as might be expected, generous in the extreme and, after the serious business had been completed, large amounts of local delicacies like sushi and tapas were consumed and washed down with copious quantities of wine and beer. By the time the single malts and brandy were circulating, the rep was already 'feeling no pain'. By contrast, when he found himself waking up in his room the next morning, his head was aching intolerably and his mouth was so dry that he had to struggle to speak.

Looking across to the neighbouring twin bed, he saw the tousled figure of his room-mate who was also just beginning to regain consciousness.

'Morning,' said the rep. 'Don't know about you, but I feel absolutely hellish.'

'Well,' grunted the other man, 'it wiz a good night.'

'Thing is,' said the rep, 'I can't remember a thing after the dinner. Was I tight?'

'Aye,' came the response, 'only the first time, but.'

YOUNG RAB was, at the risk of being undiplomatic, not the sharpest tool in the box, but he had been lucky enough to land a job at a building site through family connections. He almost blotted his copybook on his very first day by turning up for work in an old pair of wellies.

'Ye'll be awright the day,' said the foreman, 'but ye better huv a decent perr a boots this time the morra.'

'Not a problem,' was Rab's reply.

The foreman went on to ask the youth if he minded working high up on scaffolding.

'No feart a heights, are ye?'

'Nae danger, boss, Ah'm totally cool wi that.'

'Well, jump up tae the toap and tell Auld Kenny tae show ye whit tae dae. Watch it, mind, some a they bastarts'll try tae wind ye up cause ye're a new start.'

'Whit d'ye mean, boss?'

'Ah just mean they might tell ye tae go for a tin a tartan paint or somethin stupit lik that. Just keep yer wits aboot ye an don't let them take a len a ye.'

The foreman watched Rab as he made his way safely to the top of the building and saw him strike up a conversation with Auld Kenny. Satisfied that all was proceeding as it should, he turned to go about his business and was halfway across the site when he heard a sudden cry. He turned round and to his horror saw Rab leap off the building with his arms outstretched and hurtle to the ground to land with a sickening thud. He ran across to see what had happened and caught Kenny as he descended.

'What in the name a Goad did he dae that fur?' demanded the gaffer, 'did you say something tae him?'

'Nothin, boss, honest!'

'Don't come it, Kenny! Ye must've said somethin.'

'Well, Ah did mention that ma Da flew in Wellingtons during the war.'

The School

MOST OF the following stories came to me from teachers themselves and they tend to illustrate the blend of gallows humour and self-mockery that often develops amongst a group of colleagues that have to perform a difficult or pressurised job of work. Some people think teachers have it easy: a short day, and all those holidays; those with any insight into the profession know better. In any consideration of the pros and cons of the teaching profession it should be borne in mind that in the summer of 1995 a mathematics teacher at a Southside Glasgow school decided that a better option than returning in August for a new term was to sign up for a five-year hitch in the French Foreign Legion.

ONE FRIDAY night a teacher's wife was waiting for her husband to return from school. Time wore on, and the food she'd made was congealing rapidly on its plate in the oven. She began to worry; he usually came straight home from work and there had been no phone call to alert her to some other arrangement. Trying to console herself with the thought that he was a big boy now and could look after himself, she gave up watching television and went to bed. She was far too apprehensive to sleep and was still wide awake when, at 3.30 in the morning, she heard the front door open and close. She rushed into the hall and switched on the light to reveal her husband standing unsteadily, tie at an uncivilised angle, eyes all but shut, reeking of drink, the remains of a substantial night's bevvying.

'Where've you been to this time of night?' she demanded. As if it wasn't obvious. 'I thought you were coming straight home.'

The husband thought about it for a moment then his face lit up with recollection.

'I was . . . but we got away early!'

SCHOOLCHILDREN CAN be very cruel to one another, and the vulnerable period of early adolescence affords easy and ample opportunities for the unscrupulous to make a wounding remark. Who can measure the psychological scarring that may have been caused by the following jibe, overheard at a Glasgow secondary school, made by one first-year boy to another?

'Whit are *you* sayin, Baldy Baws?'

THE PRIMARY school teacher was taking pains to give her charges a good grounding in standard English. She didn't like to penalise the children for using dialect expressions in class but felt it would be doing them a disservice not to point out where they deviated from the norm of standard English.

'Children,' she began, 'Willie made a mistake just now when he said "Ah wisht Ah had goed". Now who can tell me what he should have said?'

Various hands shot up and, gratified, she chose one of the most enthusiastic volunteers.

'Miss!' cried the little girl, 'Ah wisht tae Goad Ah hud went!'

Now this teacher was not one to give up easily. She persisted in her attempts:

'And another thing: one of you said earlier that you liked to drink tea with a "wee tait" of sugar in it. If you went to England they wouldn't have a clue what you meant. Who knows what an English person would have said?'

'Easy peasy, miss!' cried an eager lad. 'A *little* tait!'

SOMETIMES THE wellie is on the other foot, as in a case I heard of in which a teacher was reprimanded by a mother for having corrected the spelling of a word in her child's essay. 'Here Ah'm tryin tae get them no tae talk in that coorse Glasgow way,' complained the concerned parent, 'An you go an cross oot the "g" in "Badmington"! In ma day teachers spoke proper. Noo some of yeez talk as rough as the weans!'

A FRENCH assistant at a local school had spent a first term getting to know her new school, the children, and the new city she found herself living in. The natives were always friendly if at times a little hard to understand, and some of their customs struck her as odd. Like students anywhere, she never had much money to play with and sometimes found it a struggle to make ends meet.

In order to help make her feel a part of things one class decided to let her take a turn with looking after the class pet. So it was with a rabbit in her care that Mademoiselle left the school for the Christmas break.

When school resumed in January one of the staff members sat next to the French girl in the staffroom. Just to make conversation she asked her:

'And how did you get on with that rabbit over the holidays?'

'Oh!' said the foreigner. 'It was delicious!'

A TEACHER was going along a tenement street on her way to the secondary school where she plied her trade. She was walking quickly, hoping to arrive in time for a cup of tea before her class. Suddenly, a small terrier-like mongrel shot out of a close-mouth and began to yap at her heels. She paused to shoo it away but the creature followed her, barking wildly. She raised her voice, employing the teacher's tone of command, but the dog seemed merely encouraged by this and began to nip at the skirts of her raincoat.

Just then a window flew up in one of the nearby flats and a woman's head emerged.

'Listen, hen,' came the voice, 'just tell the wee bastart tae f*** off.'

'I don't see any need to swear,' returned the harassed teacher, still vainly trying to shoo her persecutor away.

'Ah'm tellin ye. Ah'm no tryin tae be cheeky or nuthin, but that's the only language that wee messin unnerstauns.'

Exasperated beyond patience, the teacher gave in to this advice and, against her own habits, cried loudly:

'Oh just f*** off!'

The dog immediately stopped its yapping, gave her a look as if to say 'What's all the fuss about anyway?' and slunk off from whence it came. The teacher called a thank you to the helpful woman and sped off to school, hoping that the lady in question wasn't a parent of one of her pupils.

In a fourth-year class the next day the teacher had occasion to check one of the boys for swearing.

'Me, miss? What did Ah say?' the lad enquired, innocence personified.

'You know perfectly well what you said.'

'Ah don't, miss, honest.'

'You just told your pal next to you to "eff off".'

The boy smirked and nudged his classmate before replying:

'Oh, Ah see, miss. That's f*** off, as in "Go away, bad doggie"?'

A TEACHER of English was trying to expand the vocabulary at the command of his charges. From a list of less common words used in a recent piece of prose they were studying he made a selection. On the blackboard he chalked the word 'degrade'.

'Now,' he said, 'who's going to give me a sentence using "degrade"?'

Blank looks ensued until one boy had a brainwave.

'Sir! The Fire Degrade went flyin doon oor street!'

The teacher shook his head.

'Okay, next word.'

And he wrote up 'jester'.

It was a girl who volunteered this time.

'Ma Maw's just goat a new coffee table an a jester drors.'

ONE DAY a few years ago a teacher at a secondary school in a fairly rough area of Greater Glasgow was having a hard time. It was last period on a Friday afternoon and the pupils were as high as kites with the imminence of the weekend's freedom. Try as he might, he couldn't keep their minds on what he was trying to impart. One boy in particular was being very tiresome, speaking out of turn at every opportunity, holding personal conversations with a pal on the other side of the room. This boy ignored several warnings and the teacher eventually lost patience. He grabbed the boy, frogmarched him to a walk-in cupboard and thrust the boy in, turning the key in the lock.

'Right, you. If you can't keep quiet when you're told, you can stay in there until you can.' (I told you this was a few years ago; no teacher would dare to do such a thing these days.)

This example had the desired effect and the teacher was able to complete the lesson with a minimum of further interruption.

A couple of hours later he was in the Horseshoe Bar, sinking his third pint in a small crowd of pedagogical cronies when it occurred to him that there was something he had forgotten, some vague but persistent thought trying to reach the forefront of his brain. Suddenly, all became clear. He thumped his glass onto the bar, made cursory excuses and darted for the door. A panicky taxi-ride later, during which he had visions of his career in ruins, maybe even criminal prosecution, he arrived outside his school. He was on good terms with the janitor, who gave him access to the building after being told that the teacher had forgotten something. He rushed to his own room, unlocked the door with trembling hand and similarly the cupboard.

The boy was slumped on the floor; the teacher's heart sank.

'My God! He's suffocated! Hey! Are you okay?'

The boy's eyes opened wide and he jumped to his feet.

'Sorry, sir! Ah must've dozed aff there. Ah'm that tired wi ma paper roon an aw that!'

Relief flooding through him, the teacher strove to maintain a mask of righteous authority.

'Right. Well if you've learned your lesson you can be on your way.'

The boy's relief at not being given a punishment exercise or a referral to the head teacher was almost as great as the teacher's.

'Right, sir! Ah'll no dae it again . . . honest.'

The two of them went down to the main door.

'Ah'm away hame then,' said the boy. 'Here, it's no hauf gettin dark early, eh?'

The teacher and the janny exchanged a significant look, then the teacher dismissed the boy.

'Okay, we'll say no more about this. See you on Monday.'

The teacher went back to the pub. The boy went home reasonably contented and nothing further ensued from the incident. (See? I told you this was a few years ago.)

ONE HEADMASTER, a history specialist who often lamented the fact that his subject never seemed to engage the attention of modern children, walked into a classroom on St Andrew's Day to have a word with the teacher conducting the class. Seeing that they were discussing Mary, Queen of Scots, he immediately summoned to mind a relevant historical snippet that he felt might interest them.

'Well, class,' he said, 'did you know that Mary at one time had a pet duck that followed her everywhere?'

The class looked blank. One or two gazed at each other and shook their heads surreptitiously. The Heidie smiled, exchanged a word with the class teacher and made his exit.

'Miss,' said a boy, a puzzled frown on his face. 'No meanin tae be cheeky or that, but is he losin it? Ah mean, ma granny had a dug that followed her everywhere an aw.'

NOTES BROUGHT in by kids to explain absences can often supply gems of invention as well as misunderstandings, such as the classic note that asked the teacher to excuse this child because 'she got diarea through a hole in her shoe'.

Another mother's note explaining her daughter's absence told a sad tale of a fashion victim. Apparently the child's pierced belly button had turned septic.

AFTER A trip to Disneyworld that her parents had seen fit to take during term time a secondary school girl returned to her English class. Her teacher supplied her with a copy of the novel the class had been studying and told the pupil that as she was now a fair bit behind she should try to finish the book as soon as possible.

'Whit?' cried the girl. 'Read the hale book?'

'That's right. And why not?'

'Miss, could you no just tell us whit it's aw aboot?'

'That's not the point of the exercise. The idea is that we each read the book ourselves and then look at what there is to learn from it.'

'But that's too much bother, miss. Gauny just tell us whit happens an aw that?'

'Now you're just being silly. You have to read the thing yourself.'

'An so Ah wull. Ye canny make us read it. Ah'll get ma mammy tae you.'

The girl was as good as her word. At the next parents' night her mother turned up to see the English teacher. Her opening line was:

'Ah bet you've been tae the University an aw that, right?'

'That's right, but . . .'

'An then ye'll have done yer teacher trainin at college, willn't ye?'

'Yes, although I don't see . . .'

'An ye'll have read this stupit book she's oan aboot?'

'Of course I have!'

'Well, how in the name a the wee man can ye no tell ma lassie whit it's aw aboot? Whit're they peyin you fur anyway?'

PASSING THROUGH the playground one morning a teacher noticed a fresh piece of graffiti featuring his name: 'Doodsy says Mr Green is a toss'.

Knowing perfectly well to whom the soubriquet 'Doodsy' belonged, the teacher summoned the pupil in question to his room.

'Doodsy,' he said, more in sorrow than in anger, 'I'm afraid you've let me down this time. I thought we had established that we must respect one another.'

'But Ah do respect ye. Ah put "Mr" didn't Ah, no?'

A TEACHER in a primary school is walking around her class, which is on the ground floor, looking over the shoulders of her charges as they complete a piece of work. Her circuit takes her past the windows and she allows her glance to stray out to the world beyond. She is stopped in her tracks when she catches sight of a floppy pink item lying on the ground on the verandah just outside. She enlists the aid of one of the boys who has finished writing, asking him to go and ask the janitor to come and see her for a minute.

The janny duly appears and the teacher whispers something to him. Unfortunately, the man is somewhat hard of hearing and has to ask her to repeat what she has just said a little louder. She whispers again, with a little more emphasis, but still to no avail.

'Could ye no speak up a bit, dear?' the janny pleads.

Exasperated, the teacher gives up and announces loudly enough for not just the janitor but the whole class to hear: 'I said, there's a used condom lying on the verandah outside my window. Could you please take it away?'

With the good grace to show some embarrassment, the janitor hurries off to carry out the task. The teacher, her own face burning, turns to face the class. As she fears, a hand shoots up, its owner wearing a puzzled frown. Fearing the worst, the teacher nods,

'Yes?'

'Please, miss, what's a verandah?'

THEN THERE was the primary teacher who was keen to encourage her P6 class to abandon baby language for the more grown-up expressions they would have to use in later life. They were discussing the presents that they had got for Christmas, each child taking a turn. One little boy said,

'Santa brought me a choo-choo, miss.'

The teacher tutted.

'Now, what have I been telling you about using baby language? What you should say is "I got a model train for Christmas."'

It was a little girl's turn next.

'Miss, we got a bow-wow, a real one!'

Again the teacher corrected the child.

'Baby language again! I think what you mean is you got a new pet dog, isn't that so?'

The boy whose turn it was next had seen the way the wind was blowing and was prepared.

'I got a new book, miss, but I don't like to say what it's called.'

'Don't be silly, child. If it's suitable for you to read, it can hardly have a title you are embarrassed to tell us.'

The boy shrugged.

'OK, miss, it's *Winnie the Shite*.'

ONE BOY appeared to have real trouble with mental arithmetic. His teacher was trying him out with various sums to do in his head, but the child was defeated by all of them. Eventually, the teacher was reduced to asking the most elementary sums.

'Ok,' he said, 'we'll try a really easy one now. What's eighteen and five?'

The boy's face lit up, and for the first time he had an answer:

'Burst!'

AN OUTRAGED mother appeared at a parents' night demanding an interview with her daughter's teacher.

'Wis it you that wrote this note?' she enquired.

The teacher agreed that she had written the note.

'Well, what d'ye mean ma lassie's goat a hygiene problem?'

The teacher, slightly embarrassed, answered as best she could.

'I was just trying to put it as neutrally as possible. The thing is, some of her classmates have been complaining about having to sit next to her.'

'How?'

'You're forcing me to say it bluntly: I'm afraid she's a bit smelly.'

'Whit's that goat tae dae wi anythin? She's a lassie, no a flooer,' cried the mammy. 'She's here tae be telt, no smelt!'

A TEACHER stopped one of her pupils in the corridor and asked why he had not been at school the day before.

'Ach, Ah fell an hurt masel.'

'What happened?'

'A bunch ae us wis playin fitba an Ah kickt the baw up oan the roof ae the wee primary school so Ah hud tae go up an get it.'

'Silly boy! So you fell off the roof?'

'Course Ah did!'

'And what did you fall on?' asked the teacher, innocently trying to establish which part of the youth's anatomy had suffered damage. The boy stared at her, scorn all over his face.

'The grun of course, ya daft bitch! Whit ur you oan? An you're peyed tae teach the likes ae us!'

A PRIMARY class was watching a schools programme on biology. The subject of the day was sweat, how it occurs and what it is for. Among other things, the presenter on screen, who was English and had a rather plummy voice, explained how sweat emerges from tiny parts of the body called pores. Back in their own classroom, the pupils were quizzed by their teacher about the content of what they had seen. When she asked if anyone remembered what parts of the body sweat comes out of a little boy thrust up his hand.

'Miss! Yer paws!'

A YOUNG teacher, happy to find herself in her first long-term job, was walking along a West End street towards her flat when she noticed a dishevelled figure slumped against a wall. It was an elderly man in ragged clothes, sitting with an empty bottle of cheap tonic wine in his hand and a polystyrene cup in front of him. The cup contained a few coins, obviously placed there in the hope of attracting more. The teacher had just been paid and her heart was touched by the old man's plight. She took a ten-pound note from her purse and put it into the beggar's hand. He looked at the money with befuddled surprise for a moment then expressed his gratitude.

'Here, that's helluva generous of you, lassie. What's yer name . . . if ye don't mind me askin?'

The girl told him and he said what a lovely name it was before going on:

'And what is it ye do for a livin?'

'I'm a schoolteacher.'

'Whit!' the old man cried, obviously moved. He fumbled the ten-pound note out of the pocket where he had cached it and offered it back to his benefactor. 'Here,' he said, 'have that back. I used to be a teacher myself, an believe you me, you need it more than I do.'

Despite the young teacher's protests the old man

absolutely refused to keep the money. Eventually, she gave up and rather sorrowfully went on her way. Then he called after her: 'And by the way!' She turned and looked back to see him peering at her and heard him cry:

'Tempus fugit!'

IT WAS lunchtime at school and the weans were in the dinnerhall. One boy decided to land another in trouble. Timing his opening gambit to the approach of a patrolling teacher, he said to his victim:

'Take the "F" oot a butter.'

'Whit?'

'Take the "F" oot a butter, Ah says.'

Puzzled, the other youth could only exclaim:

'There's nae "F" in butter!'

This was just in time for the passing teacher to overhear, earning the response,

'These dinner ladies work hard enough without having to put up with your language. See me after school.'

A HISTORY lesson was in progress and the teacher touched on the subject of commerce and trade. He spoke about the way in which money came into use and showed illustrations of ancient Greek and Roman coins. In the way of revision and checking up to see what his pupils had absorbed, he posed the question:

'Now, who can remember what people used before money was invented?'

A wee girl flung up a hand:

'Was it Provvy cheques?'

AT YET another History class, the topic was the post-war period and the creation of the Welfare State. The teacher explained about the National Health Service, National Insurance, and other enlightened measures that were introduced around that time. She then threw open to the class the question of what the State had provided for elderly

people. She picked one boy who volunteered the answer:
'Bingo buses!'

AN ENGLISH teacher was working through a past examination paper with her class. Part of it involved a passage
from a Victorian novel that included the phrase: 'A
gentleman was sitting writing a letter at a desk with a
leather top.'

When the teacher asked the class to comment on
anything that seemed unusual about the piece, one girl
suggested:

'Sure the guy wouldny've been wearin a leather top in
they days.'

IT WAS Easter, and in the primary school the weans were
being told about the meaning of the Christian festival. The
teacher was perhaps laying it on a bit thick about the
Passion, with gruesome details of Jesus being beaten and
whipped, and some of the kids were becoming quite upset.
When they were told about the crown of thorns being put
on Christ's head it finally proved too much for one outraged
infant, who couldn't restrain himself from crying out:

'Aye, an where were the f***in polis when aw this was
gaun on?'

WEE DOOGIE was good at art at school, and when it came
to painting the backdrop for the school Nativity Play he
was the obvious choice to do the job. He toiled away at
his task for days, merrily absorbed in the creative act, but
he was too self-conscious to let anyone see it until he
considered it finished.

When it was finally unveiled to the teachers and kids
who were involved in the project some surprise was regis-
tered amongst the former when the painting showed Mary,
Joseph and the baby Jesus happily cruising along inside
a bright red Lamborghini sports car.

'Now, Doogie,' remonstrated one of the staff, 'It's a very

nice effort, but don't you know that they didn't have things like that in the Bible days?'

'But Miss!' protested the young artist, 'You telt me yersel that Joseph was a car painter!'

IN A Glasgow RC primary school one May morning, a teacher encountered a wee boy sitting somewhat white-faced and apprehensive outside the head teacher's office.

'And what are you doing here?' she asked him.

'Aw, miss, Ah goat pit oot fur singin.'

'What were you singing?'

'"Away in a Manger."'

'Well, apart from the fact that Christmas is well by, I don't see why singing that should land you in bother.'

'Maybe it's cos it had different words, miss.'

'Well, how about singing it quietly to me to let me see the problem?'

And in a little quavering voice, the child sang:

'Away in a manger,
No crib for a bed,
The little Lord Jesus
He sat up and said,
"Championees, Championees!
The Celts have won the Cup!"'

A SCHOOLBOY was being taken to task for yawning loudly in class.

'Are we boring you?' asked the teacher.

'Naw, miss. It's jist Ah had tae make ma bed last night.'

'Don't think you'll get any sympathy for something we all have to do every day.'

'Ah but, miss!' chipped in the offender's pal. 'He really did have tae make his bed . . . frae a flatpack his Mammy goat at IKEA!'

'WELL DONE, DARREN,' commended the teacher as she handed back a corrected essay to one of her pupils. 'That was a well-written essay, apart from one or two things you should correct.'

'What things, miss?'

'Well, as I've told you before, there are some expressions that you use in your everyday conversations that really don't belong in a formal piece of writing. For example, you said that if you met a lion in real life you would probably "shite yourself".'

'Well, so Ah would, miss. So would emdy!'

'I just think you could find a metaphor that would be less offensive.'

'That's no a metaphor, miss. Ah pure would sh . . .'

'That's enough, Darren. Not everybody would express fear in those terms.'

'Aw, miss, are you saying ye've never shat yersel?'

'Certainly not!'

'No even if ye were bein chased doon the road by a team a mad bastarts?'

'It may come to you as a surprise, Darren, but I don't spend my spare time running around the streets.'

'Christ, miss, whit dae you teachers DAE at the weekends?'

Criminal, so It Is

IN JANUARY 1996 at the High Court in Glasgow a robber who had been nicknamed The Bog Roll Bandit was sentenced to jail. Apparently he earned his soubriquet by carrying out a robbery having improvised a mask by winding a toilet roll around his head. During the trial the Advocate Depute demolished the defendant's alibi as a tissue of lies. A police spokesman denied that he was flushed with success but admitted that their task had been made easier because the perpetrator 'used a crap disguise'. He went on to bemoan the fact that this case had already generated more than the usual amount of bumf, but affirmed that the force would not slacken in its efforts to clean up this sort of crime.

A MIDDLE-AGED man who had never married and who lived with his spinster sister came home one day much agitated about a crime that had been discussed at work.

'That's terrible, that,' he said.

'What?'

'Ye know, that wummin that goat hut wi a bullet when she wis passin the bank that wis gettin robbed. Ye areny safe tae walk the streets these days.'

'Is she bad, the poor soul?'

'Well, she's lyin in the hoaspital at death's door.'

'It's a sin, so it is.'

He paused a while before going on.

'Listen, what part of a wummin's her "yet"?'

'Eh? What're ye on aboot?'

'Well, a guy at the work says the bullet's in her yet.'

AN AMATEUR burglar was roaming around the west end of Sauchiehall Street, drinking in various pubs in order to generate the Dutch courage to break in somewhere. By the time he felt gallus enough to carry out a crime he was

in no fit state to do so efficiently and blundered into the first likely-looking building. In the darkness he couldn't make out what kind of office this was and he staggered from room to room looking for anything of value with no success. He was soon feeling tired and sorry for himself and was desperate for something to eat. Eventually he came upon a set of jars containing round objects in liquid. He opened a jar and tasted the contents. Not very nice, he thought, but he continued eating until the alcohol finally overcame him and he fell asleep.

He was awakened by a couple of burly police officers and huckled out to a waiting van.

'It's no fair,' he complained. 'All I got was a jar of pickled onions. They were rotten an aw.'

The officers exchanged a grin as they escorted their captive out past the sign at the front of the building: Glasgow Eye Infirmary.

A VISITOR to the city answered a call of nature at Buchanan Bus Station. During his occupancy of a cubicle he heard a knocking from the stall next door, followed by an importunate voice.

'Hey, Jim! It's a wee bit embarrassin this, but there's nae lavvy paper in here. Any chance a slippin a wee drap through tae us?'

The visitor answered in the affirmative and, pushing his hand underneath the partition, offered a length of tissue. Whether premeditated or simply opportunist, the other man's prompt action was to stand on the helpful hand, remove the watch from its wrist, and make a quick exit before the astounded victim could react.

I WAS watching television in a bar one evening just as the news came on. The lead story concerned a kidnap case in which the victim had been released unharmed after the ransom had been paid. A large number of plainclothes police had staked out the location where the money was to be left for the kidnapper. Despite all this the criminal had managed to get away with the loot undetected. A police spokesman blamed the heavy fog for their failure to apprehend their quarry. As the item ended a wee man standing next to me (a stranger to me, who had not said a word) finished his drink and made to leave. He paused at my side and was moved to observe: 'Whit d'ye make of it, eh? Wan thoosan undercover polis watchin fur the guy. Where is he? Don't know. It wis foggy, but. Still, the lassie's hame safe, that's what's important. Money's nothin. Cheerio!'

A PICKPOCKET was plying his trade in Sauchiehall Street when he was suddenly caught in the act by a big polis. The officer was about to book the offender when he seemed to think twice about it. Saying nothing, he huckled his captive along the busy thoroughfare and round the corner and into Rose Street before getting his book out.

'Whit did ye dae that fur?' asked the puzzled delinquent.

'Ah kin spell Rose Street,' replied the lawman.

PERHAPS IT was the same police officer who, on being interviewed by a superior, maintained that he was determined to rid the city of the curse of skelp.

'What do you mean by that?' asked the senior officer.

'It's yon drug, ye know . . . aw the junkies are hooked on it.'

'Oh, I think you mean "smack".'

'Aye, that's it! Ah knew it had something to do wi hittin folk!'

I WAS told of a man who was standing in a city-centre pub when he was approached by a small boy carrying a shoebox.

'Want a perr a trainers, pal?' the child enquired. The man was feeling mellow enough to be amused by this and

asked what size they were. On being told this information, and finding that the size was right for him, he agreed
to look at them. The boy took out the left shoe and let
him try it on. The man pronounced it a good fit and they
quickly agreed on a price. The boy pocketed the money
and departed. The man took the lid off the box and after
having to shake his head and look again he saw that it
did indeed contain another left shoe.

IT WAS reported that two youths had been rushed to
hospital after taking an illicit drug that had been cut with
curry powder. Apparently one was in a serious condition;
the other was in a korma.

THE PRIME Minister was in Glasgow and came to meet
some of the asylum-seekers and other refugees who had
been allocated accommodation in the city. Through a
young lady acting as an interpreter, he asked one man
how things were.

'Not so bad. They have been very bad up to now, but
now not so bad.'

The PM told the interpreter to say that he was sure that
the poor man and his family must have endured great
hardships. The interpreter relayed the man's reply:

'Very bad. Money and valuables stolen, rapes, beatings,
living in fear at all times of day and night.'

'Dear, dear, that's very sad to hear. Please tell him he
and his family have our every sympathy.'

The translator seemed hesitant about rendering the
refugee's response to this, but after the Premier insisted
on hearing it she said:

'Sympathy is not good enough. It's your fault for putting
us into these flats in the first place.'

TWO WIFIES were having a conversation at the bingo.

1st wifie: Ye'll never guess what happened.

2nd wifie: What?

1st wifie: We got broken inty last night.

2nd wifie: Naw! That's rotten, so it is! Was there much took?

1st wifie: They goat aff wi the video, the mobile phone, and the boay's Playstation.

2nd wifie: Swine that they are! There's naebdy safe these days.

1st wifie: Ye've no heard the worst yet! Ah hud a poat a mince oan the cooker an wan them 'relieved hissel' inty it!

2nd wifie: Is that no disgustin!

1st wifie: Ah know! Ah hud tae fling the hauf ae it oot!

The Bus Conductor Whines

THE LITTLE old lady hirpled to the front of the bus, struggling to keep her balance against the vehicle's motion. When she reached the driver's coop she engaged his attention.

'Excuse me, when does this bus get to Knightswood?'

The driver didn't take his eyes from the road as he replied.

'We're no gaun tae Knightswood. We're only gaun tae Anniesland Cross.'

Outraged, the passenger protested.

'But it definitely says "Knightswood" on the front of this bus!'

'Listen, hen, it says India on the tyres but we're no gaun there either.'

BACK IN the old days when buses had conductors aboard, a wee man travelling into town from the Southside was accosted by the conductor.

'Right pal, that's your fare up at that last stop. Aff!'

'Whit d'ye mean "aff"? Ah've peyed tae the city centre.'

'That'll be right. Ye're by yer stop, so aff ye go.'

'Ah'm no gettin aff this bus till Ah get tae where Ah peyed fur!'

The conductor, maddened by this brazen fare-dodging, decided to take drastic action. He seized the passenger's suitcase and flung it through the open door of the bus. As the vehicle was crossing the King George IV Bridge at the time, the heavy suitcase sailed over the parapet and landed with a splash in the Clyde.

The passenger jumped to his feet, beside himself with rage.

'See you!' he cried. 'Not only dae ye try tae rob me, ye try tae droon ma wee boy as well!'

IT WAS a very rainy day in Glasgow's East End. On a busy bus the passengers were glad that they were not outside in the downpour. At a stop near a school, the last person to step up onto the platform was a tiny girl in a thin anorak that was obviously soaked through, its hood drawn tightly around her little head in a fruitless effort to keep her hair dry.

'Right you, aff!' said the driver.

'How?' asked the waif, plaintively.

'You know fine well there's nae weans allowed on this bus. Yeez've aw been banned fur vandalizing the buses an skippin yer fares.'

The child turned to the passengers, many of them little old ladies, to make an appeal.

'That's terrible, no lettin weans on the bus, intit, no? How'm Ah meant tae get hame in this weather? Ah've never vandalised anythin either.'

The passengers looked at the child standing there in all innocence, rain dripping from her little nose.

'That's a sin, driver, so it is,' said one lady pensioner. 'Could ye no let the wee soul on?'

A few others murmured their agreement, but the driver was adamant.

'Ah'm tellin yeez, it's company policy. These school weans're out a control. They're costin this firm a fortune wi their spray-paintin an cuttin up seats. It's mair than ma job's worth tae let a single wan ae them on.'

'Aw come on, driver. It's fair enough what ye're sayin. But could ye no make a wee exception tae get this wee lassie up the road. It's a stinkin rotten night, an ye've only tae look at her tae see she wouldny get up tae any mischief.'

The driver sighed. Being a soft-hearted man, a father himself, he relented and let the child come on. As the girl went past she gave him a long stare before sitting down. The old lady in the seat beside her was moved to ask why she had looked at the driver that way. Up spoke the child:

'Ah just want tae be able tae mind his face when Ah

get hame an tell ma big brother tae come an malky the
bastart.'

CURIOUS PASSENGER: 'Hey, driver, is this bus gaun tae
Barlinnie?'
 Bored Driver: 'Only if it disny behave itsel.'

AT A city-centre stop a drunk man, with no little difficulty, clambered aboard a bus heading for the suburbs.
He stood, swaying, at the driver's window, rifling through
various caches about his person for the necessary change.
Seeing that this might take some time, the driver chose
to move off rather than wait, with the result that the
drunk was sent flying in a scatter of loose coins. He let
out a stream of obscene oaths, cursing the driver and the
other passengers who recoiled in disgust when he came
near them. Having eventually paid his fare, the refreshed
one cast about for somewhere to sit. All eyes studiously
avoided him. He roared out fresh curses, reviling all and
sundry for everything from snobbery to hard-heartedness
to illegitimacy. One or two of the passengers began to
make representations to the driver to have this foul creature put off the bus. At this point an elderly gentleman,
well-turned-out and politely spoken, stood up and told
the man that if he wanted to sit down there was a space
next to him.
 The drunk made his way to where the good samaritan
stood, thanking him profusely, pointing him out to the
rest of the company as the only decent human being
aboard. He insisted on shaking the elderly man by the
hand protractedly before finally expressing his appreciation this way:
 'Thanks, pal. Ye're bran new, so ye ur. It's weel seen *you*
know what it's like tae be pished oot yer skull.'

ON A long-distance bus trip some of the passengers asked
the driver if he could put on a video to pass the time

away. The driver was happy enough to do this and named a few tapes that he had available. The passengers debated the merits of the films in question and after some to-ing and fro-ing decided on one that would content most of them. But before the driver could play the video one lady pointed out that the chosen film had a 15 certificate and there were a couple of children on board who were too young to watch it. Everyone was at a loss what to do about this when one man at the back suggested:

'Ach, just fill the lavvy up wi coloured balls, fling the weans in there an tell them it's a ball pool.'

HAVING APPLIED for a job as a Glasgow bus driver, a man was being interviewed by the personnel manager, who, satisfied with the applicant's driving credentials, was keen to establish if he had the right kind of temperament for this demanding work.

'What would ye dae,' he asked the aspiring driver, 'if a bunch a rowdy drunks tried tae get oan yer bus an startit giein ye cheek?'

The young man was not at all fazed by this and answered confidently, 'Ah'd tell them tae pey their money and behave theirsel or jist get aff ma bus.'

'And whit wid ye dae if they wouldny gie ye the fare?'

'Nae probs. Ah'd just take the first two weeks in July!'

A Character

THE CLINCHER was the nom-de-guerre of Alexander Wyllie Petrie, originating with his claim that he had a silver cell in his brain that empowered him to clinch any argument. Between 1897 and 1937 he wrote, published and sold his own newspaper *The Glasgow Clincher*. He was a hairdresser to trade and was not above advertising his Mount Florida salon in his paper and proclaiming the virtues of his invention 'Petrie's Golden Petals for the Hair'.

Much of the content of his paper was devoted to attacking the city Corporation and the police force, accusing the officers of both corruption and incompetence. In one typical diatribe he pours contempt on 'your lawless administrators of injustice' for 'degrading the City of St Mungo with their low passion for the essence of middle-class vulgarity, and, moreover, burdening over-taxed citizens with unnecessary taxation'.

His sniping was taken seriously enough for his enemies to attempt to silence him by having him committed to Woodilee Lunatic Asylum. The pretext, it is said, was that he had demonstrated to an alarmed customer in his barber's chair exactly how he would cut a man's throat. In the Woodilee Petrie underwent searching examination and, having proven himself nobody's fool, re-emerged with a certificate affirming his *compos mentis*. Armed with this document he was free to continue retailing his views while boasting of being 'the only certified sane man in Glasgow'.

Petrie's columns demonstrate the man's often bizarre sense of humour and his affection for gnomic observations, as in:

'You Glasgow people, for years and years you have been sending men into the Town Council who have no brains, but then you are a consistent people. You love your neighbours as yourselves.'

'Only the ugly and the stupid get through life easy.'

He also liked to make shameless claims for the excellence of his publication:

'*The Clincher* has not the largest circulation in Glasgow but it has the most intellectual readers in the world.'

'Get *The Clincher* and it will save you the trouble of going into the blues when you are coming off the booze.'

The man himself was a well-known figure on the Glasgow streets until his death in 1937. My father had boyhood memories of him, immaculate in his formal clothes and top-hat, distinguished-looking with his full white beard, selling his paper at such landmarks as The Hielanman's Umbrella. He always had a kindly word for children, and would invariably advise my father and his cronies to 'be good to your granny and give her plenty of whisky'.

The Grub

GLASGOW IS well known for the outstanding nature of the diet of its citizens; outstanding, that is, for promoting ill-health and obesity. Glaswegians have generally been adventurous enough in their eating habits though, and will try anything as long as it is deep-fried, comes with chips, and hasn't been near an uncooked vegetable. But this stereotype is changing, and there are plenty of guys out there now who are real buggers for their sushi and tiramisu. I myself, when on holiday in Europe, have been in accord with my fellow citizens when, bored with moussaka or paella, thoughts have strayed to the homely fare of our native town and we can't wait to get home for a good curry.

A YOUNG man walks into a pub and orders a pint of lager. The chargehand questions his choice of brand and points out that there is a special promotion on that night featuring a rival lager, making it substantially cheaper than the pint the customer has chosen.

'Naw,' says the young man, 'Ah'll stick tae ma usual pint.'

The chargehand is on a nice bonus if he can shift quantities of the rival lager; this makes him persevere. He has a quick and shifty glance around the bar to check if he can be overheard, then beckons the youth closer.

'Listen, what if I was to throw in a free pie and a quick trip upstairs with that gorgeous barmaid over there?'

The youth ponders a moment. He's definitely tempted, but something occurs to him.

'Haud on a minute. Whose pies are they?'

A HOME Economics teacher was giving her class a talk on the importance of healthier eating patterns. She extolled the virtues of fresh salads and particularly advised

the children not to automatically have chips with everything. Baked potatoes were a wonderful alternative, she
told them, and so versatile! You could have just about
anything you liked as a filling for a baked potato.

'Is that right, miss?' said one wee boy.

'Of course it is,' affirmed the teacher, pleased to be
getting her message across.

'Right then, Ah'm huvin baked potato an chips fur ma
dinner.'

AFTER A few pints two guys, as one does, head for the
nearest curry-shop. The waiter comes to take the order.
One of the friends says, 'See yer vindaloo here? Is it really
hot?'

'Definitely,' says the waiter. 'Our vindaloo is as hot as
they come.'

'That'll dae me then.'

'Not a wise move,' says the other guy. 'It'll be a Johnny
Cash case for you the morra?'

'What are you on about?'

'"Ring of Fire!"'

MY FATHER recalled a childhood rhyme, mocking an
advertisement of the time for a brand of sausages:

'Waddell's sausages are the best,
In the cludgie they do rest,
Pull the chain and they go west!'

A LADY went into her local butcher's to pick up some
mince. The butcher greeted her and asked how she'd
enjoyed the fine piece of steak he'd sold her the other day.

'Don't ask me,' she replied. 'That was for my husband.
I'm a vegetarian; I never touch meat at all.'

'That's too bad,' said the butcher. 'Ah hate tae think a
ma customers no bein able tae appreciate ma goods.'

'Well, there's hardly likely to be anything in a butcher's
shop that a vegetarian could appreciate, is there?'

The butcher nodded in agreement then his face lit up.

'Ye could always try wan a they Scotch pies,' he urged. 'There's bugger aw meat in thame!'

TWO WORKMATES were having their packed lunches one day. The first opened his lunchbox and brought out several corned beef sandwiches. As he set about them he noticed that the contents of his colleague's lunchbox consisted of a single boiled egg.

'That's no much ae a dinner, wan biled egg!'

His friend shrugged.

'Ah wis in that much of a hurry this mornin Ah only had time tae bile the wan.'

IT IS part of Glasgow folklore that weans playing in tenement streets or back-courts used to shout up to their mammies to fling them down a piece when they were feeling hungry. The story is told of one such incident when, instead of Milanda from heaven, the unfortunate child got a mouthful of abuse.

'Ye know fine well Ah canny make ye a piece the noo!' shouted the mother. 'Yer faither's away tae the gemme wi the breid-knife!'

SUPERMARKET BRANCHES, whether 'local' or 'express', or whatever the preferred euphemism is for 'small and having limited stock', have still not entirely replaced the traditional butchers' or grocers' shops on the suburban streets of Glasgow. It was in one of these that a wee wifie was overheard making the following order to the person behind the counter: 'See's four slices a squerr sausage . . . an nae ends!'

A DRUNK man staggers into a city-centre bakery. He struggles to focus on the display of goods behind the glass beneath the counter.

'Can I help you?' asks the young woman at the till.

'Aye, hen. Tell me this: have yeez got any hot pies?'

The girl tuts and rolls her eyes, as if to imply that it is indeed a baker's shop and it should be obvious that they will stock pies.

'We've got plenty pies,' she says, managing to bite back a withering comment. 'What kind are ye wantin?'

The customer seems puzzled by this question and it is only after a spell of hard thinking that he is able to frame a reply:

'A broon wan.'

A FRENCH tourist was being shown round The Barras by a Glaswegian friend. He found many of the stalls to be interesting, although many of the stallholders were uncharacteristically reluctant to have their photographs taken, and he even made a purchase or two. When his host suggested sampling some of the local delicacies on offer, like a portion of winkles, the Frenchman declined, saying that he was not hungry, rather than risk offending anyone by stating his real reason, which was that he thought hygiene might be an issue raised at a later time by his stomach.

As they moved towards the outer edges of the alfresco market they came across a traditional sweetshop, which made the proud boast in the window that 'All our sweets are made by hand'. The Glaswegian insisted that they should try some, like soor plooms or puff candy, as treats like those were presumably unavailable in France, but his friend replied:

'I don't mind, but can we go to a shop where they are *not* made by hand?'

No Sae Hielan as Aw That

MANY OF the merchant ships that sailed the world from the Broomielaw were crewed by Highlanders who had come to settle (when they were ashore at all) in Glasgow. My own grandfather was one of them. They have long held a place in Glasgow humour, from the immortal Para Handy to Ewan Bain's creation Angus Og, who claimed that a relation of his was 'at sea on the Whiteinch ferry'. I grew up hearing my father's stories about them, many of them hingeing on the fact that their command of English was inferior to that of Gaelic. This made them the butt of tales that the uncharitable would interpret as making them seem stupid, whereas in fact it was merely a translation problem. One seafarer in particular he called his uncle, though he was no relation but his father's great friend. His name was Dan McKinnon and he came from Tiree, but throughout the Clyde-based merchant trade he was known by his nickname. He earned this one day when the crack in the pub was about the latest improvements in the trade. Dan held forth about a new type of hydraulic crane that made loading and unloading ships a good deal easier.

'Aye,' he said, 'it's a great thing, the carbolic cran!'

After this he could only be: Carbolic Dan.

Dan was sometimes impatient of the work of other men. One of his sayings was 'I could fix it myself if I had a handful of hammers and a nail!'

One evening I was visiting my father in the Southern General hospital where he was recovering from a heart attack. We were reminiscing about Dan and my father began to tell the story involving Dan standing on a ship's deck and calling down into the hold:

'How many men's down there?'

Back came the answer:

'Seven!'

At this point an offstage voice supplied Dan's punch-line:

'Well, send the half of them up here!'

We turned to see a heavily-tattooed man in the next bed.

'Ye'll be a seagoing man yourself,' my father said.

The stranger admitted to this and went on to say that he had heard lots of stories about Carbolic Dan. He himself had crewed along with many Highland sailors; good seamen and smart, but some of them, he said, didn't think about what they said before they were saying it. He told us one about a Highlander who passed on the news that a colleague had fallen into a hold and 'broke his two skulls'. What he meant, of course, was that he had broken his skull in two places.

SIMILARLY, ANOTHER nautical Gael, when their vessel docked on the Clyde, was told by a friend that he was off into town to get a pair of jeans.

'What do you want to get two for, when one's enough for anybody!'

ONE OF the oldest Glasgow-Hielan stories concerns the young girl who leaves her native glen to walk to Glasgow in search of employment in service. Her plan is to meet up with a fellow villager who has made the same journey the year before. At the end of a weary day she comes upon a house at the roadside. She knocks at the door and enquires of the man who answers if she is in Glasgow yet. He confirms that she is. Much relieved, the girl then asks:

'Well, is Elspeth Cameron in?'

No Weel *or* Hell Mend Ye

GLASGOW IS apparently the heart-disease capital of the western world, as well as being in the top part of the league for various other life-threatening ailments. This is the fruit, we are told, of bad diet, too much smoking and drinking, and an aversion to exercise. No doubt with the latter in mind, many people have become regulars at their local gym. So busy are these that after having driven the half-mile or so to get there it fairly takes it out of you trying to find a place to park. Ah well, another clean simmit and that'll be us . . .

A YOUNG man, having heard of the recreational use of pills such as Ecstasy but having no funds to obtain any, came across some prescribed tablets in a cupboard at his parents' house. Nothing loath, he swallowed a handful and went out for a night's dancing. He duly collapsed and was rushed to hospital where his stomach was pumped. His father arrived at his bedside and minced no words in telling what he thought of him.

'Are you aff yer heid? What did ye go an swally they pills fur?'

'Ah jis thought Ah might get a wee buzz, Da.'

'Ah'll buzz ye when Ah get ye hame, ya stumer, ye.'

The youth was in no great danger but he was kept in hospital overnight for observation, being allowed only sips of water to drink and no food whatsoever. It was a very hungry young man who arrived home the next day. He took the tongue-lashing he knew was coming to him and subsided meekly into a chair in front of the television until his stomach pangs would allow him to wait no longer.

'Da,' he began, sheepishly, 'Ah'm starvin. Is there anythin tae eat in the hoose?'

The father lowered his newspaper for a moment and studied his son.

'Well,' he said, 'if ye go inty that drawer I think ye'll get a packet of aspreen.'

THE YOUNG man nervously entered his GP's treatment room. The doctor, stern-faced, told him to have a seat before saying:

'Ah've now got the results a yer tests, an Ah'm afraid the news is not so good.'

'Aw naw, doactor! Whit's the story?'

'Well, what ye're sufferin from is an advanced stage a syphilis.'

The youth was embarrassed as well as shocked.

'That canny be right, doactor!'

'Ah'm tellin ye. The tests are aw here in yer file.'

'Well, Ah don't know how Ah could a goat a thing lik that. Ah must've caught it aff a toilet seat.'

'Is that right? Well, ye must've been chowin it, cause aw yer teeth are comin oot!'

THE CONSULTANT was making his rounds at the Royal Infirmary, a posse of junior staff in his wake. They were receiving the benefit of his polished bedside manner, learning how to put patients at their ease before asking any medical questions. He approached a bed wherein lay a wee disgruntled-looking man.

'Comfy?' the doctor enquired.

'Brigton,' said the wee man.

THE FAMILY had been summoned to the hospital bed wherein lay the grandfather. They had been told that he could not last through the night, although no member of staff had actually broken the news to the patient himself, preferring to leave this sad task to a member of the family. They gathered round, a tear in many an eye, as the patriarch greeted them one by one. He had a loving word to say to each, until his gaze lit on one grandson and a malevolent light glittered in his rheumy eye:

'You here an aw, eh?' the old man said. 'You were always an ugly bastart!'

The youth was cut to the quick, having always been attached to his grandfather despite his occasional crustiness.

'Aw grandad,' he said, 'what kinna thing's that tae say when ye're dyin?'

The old man snorted:

'Dyin, am Ah? Jeez, you were always a tactless bastart an aw!'

AN OLD lady was waiting outside the Casualty Department of the Victoria Infirmary, having consigned her husband, who had slipped on a patch of ice and injured his arm, to the care of the staff. It seemed to her that a long time had passed and she began to worry that something might be amiss. She asked at the reception window if she could talk to a doctor, only to be told, kindly but firmly, that everything possible would be done for her husband and that when there was anything to report she would be first to know. This pacified her for a few minutes but her fears resurged. Deciding she would get no joy from the receptionist, she resolved to accost the first doctor she saw emerging from the treatment area. There was a fair amount of coming and going but none of the staff she saw appeared to fit the bill.

At last a person in a white coat appeared and she moved towards him. When she got closer she realised that this was a rather young man and that he had extremely long hair.

'Canny be a doactor,' she thought to herself. 'But mibby he's a student doactor. He might know something if he's a student.'

The white-coated youth was making for the exit when the lady blocked his path.

'Excuse me,' she said. 'Would you be comin oot for a doactor?'

The youth shrugged and replied,
'No me, missus. Am comin oot fur a fag.'

THEN THERE was the man who arrived late for work one morning. On being asked by a colleague why this was, he laconically replied:
'Ma aul man goat burnt.'
'Oh dear,' sympathised the colleague. 'Was it serious?'
'Oh aye,' was the reply. 'They don't fart aboot at that cremmy.'

TWO MEN were in an off-licence, obviously seeking to further stoke up what was obviously already a substantial head of steam. One, visibly swaying, is peering at the price-tickets on the shelves and plainly having difficulty. He puts one hand over his face and says to his companion:
'Oh man! See ma eyes? They're gettin worse, so they are.'
His pal is less than sympathetic, gives him a bleary look before resuming his own inspection of the merchandise. His only comment is:
'Well, ye know whit they say: if they're bad get them oot.'

A HEAVILY-BUILT woman came out of her doctor's surgery on the point of tears. Her friend, who was waiting outside for her, promptly asked whatever was the matter. Gulping back a sob the patient managed to say:
'It's whit that doactor said tae me. He said that Ah wisny jist overweight, Ah wis clinically obese!'
Her friend was outraged.
'The cheek a him! He's goat nae right tae talk tae ye lik that.'
'Ah know. Ah wis pure gobsmacked.'
'Ah mean, Ah know ye like a good feed an aw that, but Ah wouldny say ye were a beast!'

The Toon Cooncil

THE CITY of Glasgow has always had a council full of lively incident and characters. After all, this was the scene of a Conservative councillor using the relatively uncommon technique of hiding up a chimney in order to be present at a meeting to which he was not in receipt of a formal invitation. The fact that a local nickname for a council meeting is The Fiddlers' Rally is an indication of how representatives of local government are often perceived.

HOW MANY Glasgow councillors does it take to change a lightbulb?

Twenty-one. One to actually change the bulb but only after a party of twenty has been to Florida to investigate best practices currently in favour in US local government.

BACK IN the old days when municipal corruption was a byword in Glasgow, a man was leading a horse and cart through a city-centre street looking for a particular address. When he found the place he was looking for he looked around for a lamp-post where he could tie up the animals' reins. Finding nothing immediately suitable, he thought he would ask for the help of a well-turned out passer-by.

'Would ye mind ma horse an cart while I go a wee message?' he asked. 'I'll only be a minute.'

The other man turned red, then white with anger.

'Do you know who you're talking to?' he spluttered. 'Don't you realise I'm a Glasgow Bailie?'

'Is that a fact?' said the carter. 'But surely tae Goad Ah can trust ye wi ma horse an cart for five minutes?'

AT A council meeting the worthies were discussing public transport. The last item on the agenda was the case of a particular bus service with a slight problem.

'It seems there is an unaccounted-for monetary deficit

in the region of fifteen pound,' one representative told the meeting. 'The question is: what are we going to do about this?'

There was much wagging of heads but no answers were forthcoming until one councillor was emboldened to suggest, 'Eh, could we no jist gie it tae the driver?'

HOW CAN you tell when a councillor isn't telling you the truth?

You can see his lips moving.

THE STORY is told of a Glasgow Bailie in the 1830s who was one of a delegation sent to Paris by the city to congratulate Louis Philippe on gaining the throne of France. The King graciously invited the party to dinner and after the meal they retired to the library for brandy and cigars. The Bailie in question was asked by the monarch what his profession was and he replied that he was a bookseller. The king led him to his bookshelves and pointed out the many volumes there by celebrated British writers. The king picked out a volume of the works of Burke, praising its particularly fine binding. On hearing the author named, the Bailie, who knew of only one Burke, notorious for his partnership with Hare, cried out:

'The villain! Ah wis there when he wis hanged!'

THE COUNCIL Direct Works Department received a call from an irate pensioner complaining about one of their workmen. The old lady in question had not long moved in to her high-rise flat and had been having a look around at the view. According to her, when she'd first looked out that morning a council painter had been at work on the railings inside the grounds of the chapel across the way. The next time she'd had a peer around she thought he hadn't made much progress. But at lunchtime when she'd checked on him she'd finally realised that he was hardly any further forward at all! The whole thing was a scandal,

what with the Council Tax, good men out of work, and this fellow idling. A member of staff agreed to look into the matter. He would personally head for the chapel she mentioned and see what was going on. It was with some satisfaction and relief that he was later able to report to the concerned citizen that the 'council painter' was in fact a statue of Jesus blessing children.

TWO FRIENDS were watching a martial arts epic on video. After watching one particularly severe blow administered with the back of a fist, one of the viewers observed to the other:

'Did ye see the backhander he gave him there? That guy must work for the council.'

AS GLASGOW continues to levy ever-increasing amounts of Council Tax from its ever-decreasing population, some cynics say that its citizens are perfectly justified in wondering if the old song 'I Belong to Glasgow' has taken on a new and different level of meaning.

THE BRAND new sports centre in the Gorbals wasn't open long before it became very well used. A women's yoga group soon became a regular fixture in one of the gyms on the ground floor. One evening the class was in session when one of the janitors began painting a black band around the foot of the floor-length windows, up to about four feet in height, effectively making that part of the glass opaque. As she took a break for a cooling drink, the class teacher asked the jannie what was going on, observing that it was a shame to block out the view.

The jannie, without ceasing his brushstrokes, replied, 'Aye, well, it's no ma idea, hen. Ah'm only carryin oot orders.'

'But why is this necessary?'

'It's because of aw the complaints aboot the berr arses.'

The teacher was affronted.

'Bare arses! There's no bare arses in my class or any other that I know of.'

The jannie shook his head.

'Naw, missus, ye've got it the wrang way roon. It's tae stoap aw they wee boays moonin in at ye.'

AN EMPLOYEE in the Culture and Sports department was asked by her line manager to explain a particular item in her submitted accounts for the preceding tax year.

'What's puzzling me,' he said, 'is this item about a fee for a cherry picker . . .'

'Whit's the problem?

'I wasn't aware that the City Council was growing any cherries, let alone needing to hire someone to harvest them.'

The employee coudn't help but laugh.

'No disrespect, but it's no that kind of cherry picker. It's a mechanical lifting platform that lets ye access high-up things.'

'I knew that, of course I did. I was just kidding . . .'

'Aye, right,' she muttered.

'What was that?'

'Nothing!'

'Anyway, I still don't get it. What does the Culture and Sport department need one of these cherry pickers for?'

'Oh, it's to do with the Museums side.'

'What museum?'

'The Glasgow Museum of Modern Art.'

'What is it, an installation of some sort?'

'Kind of. Aye, I suppose ye might say that.'

'Give me the details, please, before I lose my patience.'

'Well, you know the Duke of Wellington statue ootside the GOMA?'

'Of course.'

'Well, ye know how it's always got a red-and-white traffic cone on its heid?'

'I have noticed, yes.'

'Ye know how it wis dead windy last month? Well, the cone got blew aff and we used the cherry picker tae pit it back oan again.'

Animals – Do We Care What They Say?

ONE EVENING at the Brownies, a discussion about pets was in progress.

'What about dogs?' said Brown Owl, helping things along. 'Has anybody got a dog?'

Various wee girls spoke about their canine companions until one Brownie let them all know that the family pet in her house was a pit-bull terrier.

Brown Owl was surprised and a little concerned.

'Aren't they quite dangerous to have in the house?'

'Naw,' said the girl. 'Oors is dead saft. He barks a lot an that but it's aw talk wi him.'

Brown Owl persisted.

'But no matter how docile they are they can turn on you just like that and give you a terrible bite. It's against the law to take one out in the street without a muzzle.'

'Oors wid never bite emdy.'

'How can you be sure. Does it wear a muzzle?'

'Naw, the ol man says he wisny peyin good money for a muzzle an jist punched aw its teeth oot.'

A MAN is waiting at a bus stop, leaning against a handy wall, casually eating a pie supper. A lady appears, accompanied by a wee nyaffy dog which is not on a lead. The animal's interest is soon attracted by the tantalising odour of the man's meal and it begins to make a nuisance of itself by jumping up at his hands. The diner patiently waits for the dog-owner to impose some decorum on the creature but no such action is forthcoming. Instead she pretends not to notice what is going on. The man shrugs and taps the lady on the shoulder.

'This your dug?' he enquires.

The lady eyes him suspiciously but nods.

The man goes on.

'Can I throw it a wee bit?'

The lady's face brightens at discovering a fellow dog-lover and she tells him,

'If you want.'

So he lifts the dog with one hand and throws it over the wall.

A WHITE horse trots into a pub in Argyle Street, makes its way up to the bar and says,

'A pint of eighty-shillin, please.'

The barstaff, not to mention the punters, are somewhat taken aback and nobody can get their jaw shut to make a reply.

The horse whinnies in impatience.

'A pint of eighty, Ah says. An make it a straight glass.'

The chargehand snaps out of it first and manages to find his voice.

'Right away, big yin,' he says, pouring. 'Sorry aboot the delay an that. It's just we don't see many of your kind in here.'

'Ah'm no surprised,' observes the horse. 'The service is mingin.'

The pint poured, the barman asks,

'How is it ye wantit a straight glass by the way?'

The horse grips the tumbler with its teeth and tips the pint straight down its throat.

'Are you daft?' it asks. 'Tae the likes o me a haunle oan a gless is aboot as much use as an ashtray oan a motorbike. Same again.'

A boozer standing at the bar nearby decides it's safe to stick his oar in.

'Hey, pal,' he says to the horse, 'know what's amazin? There a boatle a whisky oan that gantry that's named efter you.'

'Whit?' says the horse, 'Shuggie?'

A COUNCIL workman entered the front garden of a block of flats, having been assigned to trim the communal hedge. He was about to begin work when a large mongrel dog, obviously a male, appeared with a tennis ball in its jaws. It immediately dropped the ball in a meaningful manner and began to bark loudly. The workman told the creature to go away and let him get on with his job, but the dog continued to bark, louder if anything. He tried ignoring it but its importunateness merely increased and it began to nip at the ankles of his overalls.

At this point a top-floor window opened and an old lady leaned out. She called to the workman over the barking:

'Kick its baw, son! Otherwise it'll no gie ye a wink a peace.'

The workman shook his head and shouted back:

'Naw, no way, missis!'

The lady insisted:

'Ah'm tellin ye. Ah know that dug. Ye'll need tae kick its baw, son.'

'Okay, missis,' the man conceded, 'but it wis your idea, right?'

The dog had stopped its barking and had turned away from the workman to look up at the old lady. Its tail wagged merrily as the workman stepped back, took aim for the fork between its hind legs and swung his heavy rigger's boot.

HAVE YOU ever wondered which animal would win in a fight between a pit-bull terrier and a shark? Perhaps not. I was told the story of a family living in a flat in one of the schemes who, not content with owning one of these dogs, bought a small shark. The fish was installed in the flat in its own aquarium, under the baleful eye of the dog. The father warned the children not to leave the dog alone in the room with the shark; pit-bulls were well known to be jealous beasts and there could be trouble. The weans duly noted this instruction but, being weans, duly ignored it. So it was that the father returned home one day to find the tank overturned and, in the middle of a soaked carpet, dog and fish having a square go. The father separated the combatants and managed to get the shark back into some water. Neither animal seemed mortally injured but the man felt he should have a vet look at the fish's wounds. I'm sure that made for an interesting day at the surgery. Who won? You'd have to say the pit-bull, having the advantage of its own environment. An encounter in the sea would no doubt have a different result.

AT ONE Glasgow school there operates a Careers Officer with a particularly wicked sense of humour. One girl in particular was always pestering him to arrange some work experience for her. When asked what it was she wanted to do her reply was always the same:

'I want to work with animals.'

The girl was delighted when he told her that he had managed to get a local firm to agree to let her come and try out a job with them. She wasn't so happy when she saw the name of the company: Rentokil.

THE STAFF of a nursery school in Castlemilk planned to teach the little ones in their care about how things grow by letting them plant their own seeds and watch as the flowers emerged. A piece of spare ground that was available was accordingly dug up and the earth carefully turned over by council workmen one Friday afternoon, in preparation for planting on the following Monday.

Monday morning found the staff and children assembled at the freshly-dug area with the packets of seeds to be planted. The kids were issued with little spades to dig suitable holes and told to get started. Almost immediately a wee boy called to one of the nursery nurses:

'There's somethin in this grun,' he said, frowning. 'It looks like a dug's heid.'

The adult dug away more earth and was soon able to confirm that there was indeed a dead dog under a shallow layer of soil.

'I think we'll maybe finish this after,' she said, and rounded up the kids. Later excavations unearthed another couple of expired canines, a tortoise and a budgie. It seemed that over the weekend nearby flat-dwellers who had noted the turned-over earth had been unable to resist it as a ready-made disposal place for their deceased pets.

AN EAST End schoolboys' version of the tale of *Goldilocks and the Three Bears* . . .

Daddy Bear: Somebody's been eating my porridge!

Baby Bear: Tae hell wi yer porridge, somebody's stole the video!

ONE DAY in early November the mother of a large family in Springburn came to the painful decision that the family pet, a black cat, had so many things wrong with it that it would be better to have the creature put out of its misery. It bore the scars of many a back-court fight, not the least of which being the lack of one eye, and was covered in lumps and sores. Not having the money to pay a vet to have the cat humanely put down, it seemed as if the only option was the traditional one of drowning it in the canal. When the idea was put to the assembled children none of them was happy with the idea and there were no volunteers to carry out the dark deed. The only way that the mother could see out of this impasse was to collect what money could be spared and offer it to a vet in the hopes that the practitioner's sense of charity would allow him to absorb the rest of any cost.

A family whip-round was organised, pockets and purses were turned out, and the sum of £1.85 was realised. This was put in an envelope and offered to anyone with the fortitude to take on the sad errand. As before, there were no takers until one of the younger kids, a seven-year-old boy, piped up that he would do it. He was congratulated on being a good brave boy and was given the money along with a ventilated boot-box tied with string that contained the doomed animal. The bold lad set off, saying that he would go out with his pals later instead of coming straight home, and was gone the rest of the day.

It was with some surprise that the mother, first up the next morning, confronted the sight of the black cat sitting on top of the cooker, next to the open kitchen window, looking a little damp but contentedly sticking its paw into the chip-pan and licking off the fat. The seven-year-old was summoned; he denied everything. Only after intensive cross-examination did he break down and confess that he had tossed the package in the canal and spent the money on fireworks. It wasn't fair, anyway; all his pals could get bangers except him, and the cat was for the off anyway. Over the subsequent fates of boy and pet it would be best to draw a veil.

A PARTY of secondary school children from Possil was having a trip to a wildlife safari park. All was going well until, after a quick head-count, one of the teachers in charge noticed that two boys were unaccounted for. A search commenced and, to the horror of the teachers and the safari park employees, it was discovered that the boys had somehow clambered over the fencing and into the lions' enclosure. Emergency measures went into operation. Keepers armed with tranquiliser guns supervised the removal of the lions into another caged area and the youths out of the enclosure. The boys were confronted with exasperated teachers, furious park staff, and stern-looking policemen. As they faced the music, one of the boys resentfully observed:

'It's no fair. We never even touched yer f***in lions!'

IT'S A freezing cold day, or a beezer as we say in these parts, and a frog and a toad are making their way along a road. So viciously cold is it that the toad suffers the fate of the proverbial brass monkey but he is so numb that he doesn't notice what has dropped from his person onto the ground. Helpfully, the frog tries to draw his companion's attention to his loss, saying:

'Want yer baws, Toad?'

After a moment's puzzled reflection the toad replies:

'Want yer arse kicked?'

Pure Observational, Intit?

GLASWEGIANS TEND to be adept at a quick summary of a person's appearance and often turn this into an amusing comment, or, with that little extra edge, a swift and scything put-down. Like the Colt 45 of the Wild West, a sharp sense of humour can be an equaliser, allowing many an apparent underdog to win the day by words alone. The best of friends are often given to slagging each other rotten. But it's all in good fun; they're only kidding . . . sometimes.

ONE OF the earlier examples of this type of humour is to be found in the pages of *The Brave Days*, a collection of memoirs by the author Neil Munro, most famous for his Para Handy stories. The writer describes an incident in his youth (around the 1870s) when he was involved in a parade by a volunteer company of Glasgow Highlanders. He thought he looked the picture of martial splendour in his kilted uniform but was somewhat deflated by a remark made by a woman in the crowd as they marched along the Trongate:

'"Oh, Mery!" she exclaimed at the moment I came abreast of her, "here's an awfu' peely-wally yin!"'

RANALD MCCALL told me a story involving his girlfriend, who is given to wearing lipstick of a vibrant red colour. Ranald was working on the design of a bar when he decided to have a break. When he came back one of the staff accosted him.

'Eh, there wis a bird here lookin fur ye.'

'Oh, who was that?' Ranald asked.

'Didny catch the name,' said the guy, 'but she had a mooth lik a twin-bar fire.'

THEN THERE was the youth who was considered over-thin:

'He's barely six stone wringin wet.'

THE BALD-HEADED man who was renowned for head-butting:
'He's got a heid lik a gas boatle.'

THE YOUNG lady whose make-up failed to win the approval of a male observer:
'She looks lik she pit her lipstick oan wi a lavvy brush.'

THE UNFORTUNATE individual with the acne-scarred face:
'He looks like he's been dookin fur aipples in a hot chip-pan.'

THE SKINNY youth who turned out for a game of five-a-side football:
'Last time Ah seen legs like that there was a message tied tae wan a them.'

THE LADY with a long and sharp nose:
'The last time Ah clocked a nose like that it wis openin mulk boatles.'

THE LESS-THAN-ADONIS-LIKE young man:
'When he wis born he wis that ugly the doactor skelped his mammy.'

YET ANOTHER youth who is definitely not one of the beautiful people: 'He's that ugly they gave him the copy-right on ugliness. Every time emdy that's even a wee bit ugly goes oot in public they need tae pey him royalties.'

THE CLASSIC suggestion of ugliness on the part of the addressed individual:
'What're you gauny dae for a face when King Kong wants his arse back?'

OVERHEARD BETWEEN two young men, one obviously the worse for wear:

'Whit a state ye're in, man. Ye look lik sumdy in a bad disguise!'

I HEARD of what a young man thought was a good chat-up line to the girl he was dancing with at a disco:

'Ye don't sweat much fur a fat girl!'

MY FATHER once worked beside a man who was known to all and sundry as Subway. This wasn't because he had a penchant for this mode of travel but because his piggy nose never failed to put people in mind of the Underground's twin tunnels.

A YOUNG lady was walking along Sauchiehall Street, feeling quite pleased with herself in her new silver dress. She saw a couple of small boys on the other side of the street stop and whistle at her. She took this in good part as a piece of harmless fun until she heard one of the boys cry after her:

'Hey, doll! Ye look like the inside of a vacuum flask!'

WHILE DRIVING along Pollokshaws Road one afternoon I came to a halt at a red traffic light immediately behind a particularly dirty Transit van. I noticed that it had the customary finger-scrawlings marked in its dust and, as one does in these situations, I idly read them. What I saw wasn't the banal 'wash me' or 'also in white'. What the moving finger had writ was: 'Washed by Stevie Wonder, Driven by Boy Wonder.'

TWO YOUNG ladies in a night-club found themselves being eyed up by a lounge lizard. Nothing remarkable in that, but this one was well past his sell-by date and was wearing an obvious toupee. One girl turned to the other and remarked,

'Have ye clocked God's gift over there?'

Her friend gave the man a quick up-and-down look of appraisal then delivered her judgment,

'I think he's a wee doll,' she said.

The first girl was aghast.

'Eh?' she cried. 'How d'ye make that out?'

'Easy,' said the second girl. 'His hair's pasted on!'

A CROWD of workmates are having a few drinks together when one of them begins to become boastful about his love life.

'Ye wanty've seen this bird Ah nipped the other night. She wis lik a movie star.'

'Aye we know,' says a sceptic on behalf of them all, 'she wis the double of Danny De Vito.'

SPEAKING OF movie stars, I was told of a young man who had just sat an examination and felt that he had not been successful. 'Ah've got two hopes of passin that,' he told a friend who asked how he'd got on. 'Bob Hope an nae hope!'

AT A party one evening, a vertically-challenged young man was chatting up a taller woman, as is often the case. Obviously believing he might be getting somewhere, he was bold enough to put the direct question:

'Fancy coming back to my place, doll?'

The woman looked loftily down on her suitor, then replied:

'Naw, why don't you come back to mine? You'd look great on my mantlepiece.'

AT ONE of Glasgow's many public parks a party of visiting dignitaries from a local authority in England was being given a guided tour. As the tour came to an end, one of the park-keepers, already fed up at being lumbered with the extra duties this visit entailed, was hailed by one of

the visitors, an exceedingly overweight man, in a peremptory manner:

'You there! Can I get out through that gate over there?'

Looking up and down the other man's portly figure, the parkie replied:

'Ah don't see why no. A bin-lorry made it through this mornin.'

A COUPLE of years ago I went with a friend to the Barrowlands Ballroom to see a concert by BBM, i.e. Jack Bruce, Ginger Baker, and Gary Moore. My friend and I had both been fans of Cream since our schooldays and were close enough to the stage to see that Bruce and Baker were in reasonably good nick for 50-plus, although it had to be said that Baker was looking the more timeworn of the two. We were delighted when the band played some of the old classics like 'Sitting on Top of the World' and 'Sunshine of your Love'. On the latter number Bruce actually gave up singing and let the audience do it for him. As usual at these gigs the band played a 'last' song before being summoned back for the statutory encore. Bruce and Moore appeared together and picked up their instruments. Baker did not immediately follow and the other two checked their tuning while they waited. Still the drummer didn't come onstage. The two guitarists exchanged a word then launched into the opening bars of 'Politician' without him. Baker then walked on to ironic cheers from the audience, paused at a microphone and said he had just been having 'a nice cup of tea'. The crowd laughed and there were a few cries of 'Aye, that'll be right!', then my friend said to me, 'No way. He was gettin a new battery in his pacemaker!'

ONE FESTIVE season I found myself at a party given by a graphic design firm in their premises near Park Circus. It was a fairly prestigious address and their spacious studios were located at basement level. Professional caterers had been hired to supply and serve food, and among the hospitable range of refreshments available was a particularly expensive brand of imported lager, only available in cans. I was talking to a designer from a neighbouring firm who explained that he had left his colleagues working to finish a rush job.

'I told them I was going to a party, and they called me a lucky bastard. And here I am drinking a tin of beer in a dunny!'

A STRANGER in a city-centre bar was plainly shocked at the price of his pint. As he handed over his money he told the barman:

'You should be wearin a mask, pal.'

YOU WOULDN'T want to be the object of this remark:

'Ah'm no sayin Ah don't like the guy, but if he snuffed it Ah'd take a kerry-oot tae his funeral.'

IN SOME of Glasgow's far-flung housing schemes amenities may be few and far between, and the mobile shop is a godsend to many residents. One such shop was doing business on a Friday afternoon when a wee boy was next to be served.

'A half-pun a bacon, six rolls, and four toilet rolls,' he requested of the shopkeeper, who duly supplied the order.

On the following Monday morning the same wee boy appeared at the shop, clutching an unopened pack of two toilet rolls.

'Hey, mister,' he said to the shopkeeper, 'ma mammy says kin we get the money back on these toilet rolls and get a loaf a breid an at?'

'What's up, son,' asked the shopkeeper, drily yet not unkindly. 'Did yer visitors no turn up?'

AT THE opening of an exhibition in Castlemilk I was talking to Seoras Wallace of the Wallace Clan, who specialise in re-creating the costume and combat of Highlanders for films. He told me that as he and a companion, both fully rigged out in belted plaids and weapons, were making their way on foot to the exhibition, their approach drew the following comment from a wee local boy:

'Err they c***s fae *Braveheart*.'

A LADY of a certain age was struggling away from a supermarket checkout with several bulging carrier bags when a youth in the store's uniform approached her, smiling ingratiatingly.

'Would you like me to give you a hand with these, dear?' he enquired.

The lady looked him up and down with unconcealed disdain.

'Don't call me "dear",' she told him frostily. 'I've got coats in my wardrobe older than you, and I'm wearing one of them.'

TWO OLD worthies were having a chat over a pint in their local. One took out of his pocket a smart new mobile phone.

'See that?' he said to his pal. 'D'ye know how tae work it? Ma daughter bought me it but it's as much use tae me as a chocolate watch'

His crony squinted at the device and shook his head.

'Naw, canny help ye there. Ah've never hud wan a they things an Ah'm no gauny stert noo.'

'Evrubdy's goat wan noo, even ma grandweans. Ye canny get away fae them.'

'Ah know. It's because a them that ye don't know where ye are these days.'

'Whit d'ye mean?'

'In the auld days if sumdy wis walkin alang the street shoutin inty his haun ye knew he wis a loony!'

What Other Places?

GLASWEGIANS ARE often criticised for acting as if their city is the centre of the universe, as if everywhere else must necessarily be inferior. The criticism is justified up to a point, as is the Glasgowcentricity when you look at some of the competition. Glasgow humour reflects this disdain for everybody else's home town, as some of the following examples will show.

EDINBURGH, WHICH many love to twin with Glasgow in mutual resentment, is traditionally dismissed as characterised by 'fur coat and nae knickers' and as the place where the hospitality only extends as far as saying to guests: 'You'll have had your tea.'

Paisley, being a near neighbour, comes in for plenty of stick, such as in the Glaswegian nickname for a hammer: a Paisley screwdriver. Another remark, perhaps dating from the era when Paisley's cotton mills were full of female workers, stigmatises a man as particularly ugly when it is said that: he couldny get a wummin in Paisley.

Of Aberdeen: 'What do Aberdonians call a sheep tied to a lamp-post? A leisure centre.' Others maintain that the true meaning of the term 'Highland Clearances' is what happens on the streets of Aberdeen on a flag day.

As far as Lanarkshire is concerned, I once heard the cruel remark: 'Ah start countin the weans' thumbs when Ah get the length a Lanark.'

When I started school in a city-centre secondary there was one youth who didn't come from Glasgow itself but from Hamilton. Most of us weren't too sure where that was, but as that was the day when nicknames were being freely handed out, the poor lad subsequently went through five years of being known as 'Country Boy'.

A FRIEND of mine, let's call him Bob, loved to holiday

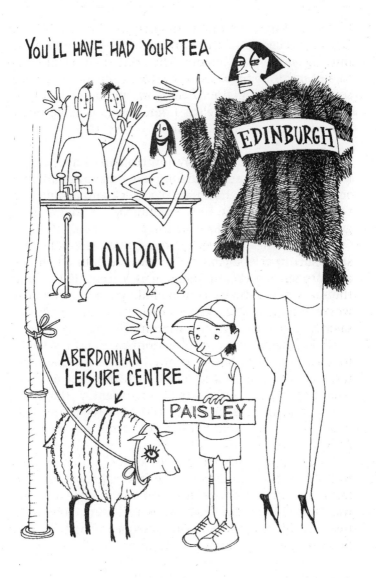

abroad and had travelled all over Europe, even visiting Canada and the USA by the time he was in his mid-twenties. Like many a Glaswegian, however, his acquaintance with the rest of Scotland was minimal and he used to take plenty of slagging for this from friends who were into climbing and hillwalking north of the Highland Line. The furthest north Bob had ventured was Milngavie. Deciding it was time he saw a little more of his native land, he asked those in the know what would be a good place to visit up north. Some said Skye, others Ullapool; Bob decided on Mull.

He rose early one Saturday morning and caught a train up to Oban. The scenery of the West Highland Line was mostly hidden from his view by a thick curtain of rain. It was pouring in Oban too, and he made sure of getting on the first available ferry to Mull. He wandered the deck of the vessel for a minute or two until the drizzle forced him below to the bar, where he consoled himself with a pint. Disembarking at Craignure, he went for a look around, failing to realise that the bus he managed to miss was his only way, other than walking, to get to Tobermory where he had planned to stay for the night. Noticing a hotel, he reckoned it would do to get out of the rain while waiting for the next bus. In the bar he ordered a pint and peeled off his streaming cagoule for the first time in what seemed like hours. The barmaid was friendly, the open fire was warm and welcoming, and the beer wasn't bad at all. Bob was content for the first time that day and happily stood at the bar until he became aware of an insistent hunger.

He asked the barmaid if they did food and was promptly shown a menu of very acceptable fare. He climbed onto a bar stool to eat and ordered another pint. Replete at last, he washed the meal down with another beer and accepted the invitation of some local lads to join in a friendly game of darts. While on the way to the toilet, he looked out of a window: it was still pouring down outside.

A few more pints later, Bob began to feel a little fatigued. He asked the barmaid if they had any rooms. On being assured one was available, he reserved it, had a nightcap and retired to bed. The next morning it was bucketing down outside. Bob compared the situation to a game of soldiers, checked out, took the ferry back to Oban and the train to Queen Street. That night he was back in his local, telling everybody that, as he had now done the Highlands, he wanted to hear no more about the matter.

TOURIST: EXCUSE me, please can you direct me to the Burrell Collection?

Old Keelie: You a German an that?

Tourist: I am from Germany, yes.

Old Keelie: Well ye managed tae find Clydebank wi yer bombers in the Blitz. Ye can find the Burrell yersel.

Another German tourist was wandering along Dumbarton Road, no doubt in search of the Kelvingrove Gallery, when she spotted a local mother giving a child a skelp. She tut-tutted and remarked to the woman:

'In Germany, we do not hit children.'

'Zat right?' came the reply. 'In Partick we don't gas Jews.'

GLASWEGIANS DO get about and they turn up all over the world. They tend to hold on to their roots, though. I heard about a computer program in America that its creator had called 'jimmy'. Not only that, but apparently the password needed to access the program was 'cu jimmy'. I think that rather tends to give the game away as to this particular computer-nerd's origins.

LONDON HAS always been a magnet for Glaswegians seeking a wider experience of life (or just a job), even though you can't always get square sausage down there. I was told this tale by one of a pair of friends, in disparagement of the other. It seems that when they were both sixteen they decided it would be a gallus thing to do to hitchhike to London, at least for a jaunt, maybe for good if things worked out. They made it to the Big Smoke and met a friendly fellow Glaswegian who invited them to spend the night in the squat where he was living. During the night one of them got up to go to the toilet. When he entered the bathroom he was surprised to find two men and a woman sharing a bath. They were hospitable enough to invite him to join them. And what did this would-be gallus man of the world, on the road for the first time, find to say?

'Eh . . . Ah'm only sixteen an ma mammy telt us tae wait tae Ah got merrit.'

ONE DAY at Hampden Park, when it still had its terracing, an important match was in progress. At one point a fan saw a nearby member of the crowd turn away from the action and bow his head.

'What's up wi him?' he asked his friend. 'Imagine comin tae a big game lik this an turnin yer back oan it.'

His friend looked round briefly before observing:

'Ah suppose it's because he's a furriner.'

'Eh? How'd ye work that out?'

'He's a Filla-peein!'

AN ENGLISH tourist was being shown to his lodge in the grounds of an exclusive hotel near Loch Lomond by a Glaswegian member of staff. The stranger looked around with an air of contempt:

'The grounds are not exactly extensive, are they?'

'They're big enough, we find, sir.'

'I hardly think so. At home in Surrey it takes me all of forty minutes to drive from the gates to the front door.'

'Aye, Ah used tae have a motor lik that an aw.'

I WAS told the story of a Glasgow man who decided to spend a holiday on the Isle of Barra. It was to be his first visit to the island but he had been told it was a lovely and hospitable place. In company with a couple of pals, he duly set off on the overnight ferry from Oban. When it grew too dark to admire the passing scenery they passed much of the evening in the bar, and being on their holidays they didn't stint the pints. So it was with rather a woozy perception the next morning that the Glaswegian looked out of his cabin porthole just as the vessel was coming into harbour in Castlebay. As they passed beneath the towering structure of Kisimul Castle he turned to his pals and observed:

'Hey, Ah didny know they hud tenements in Barra!'

JUST TO show there's no hard feelings, here's a joke they tell in Edinburgh against Glaswegians.

How do you make a Ouija board?

Take away his jellies and his mobile phone.

A GLASWEGIAN-born emigrant came back from Canada on holiday and in between visits to various relatives decided to go for a walk by himself through his native Bridgeton to see what remained of the old familiar sights. He found that some of the old street names were still there but that in most cases remembered buildings no longer stood where they once did. There were whole areas of new housing with names like 'Something Gate' or 'Such and Such Manor' that were not only new but seemed somewhat out of place. Imagine his delight when he came across a lone pub, the only remnant of a former tenement block, that he recognised from the old days. He strode in and ordered a half and soon was engaged in conversation with another old-timer who was propping up the bar. The visitor explained that he had once lived in the area and began to reminisce. The local man was happy to share memories.

'D'ye mind wee Davie McPherson?' he asked.

The Canadian shook his head.

'Can't say I do.'

'But he lived here then, just roon the coarner fae here, next door tae the Mulvaneys.'

'Don't know them either.'

'Away! Everybody knew the Mulvaneys. The auld man wis a big polis and their youngest boay wis at school wi me an Josie Stubbs.'

The visitor was obviously puzzled.

'Who's Josie Stubbs?' he said.

'Ye don't know Josie? Wait a minute, pal. Are ye *sure* ye're fae Brigton?'

ONE MORE fling at Edinburgh never goes amiss. A Kelvinside lady was visiting her cousin in Morningside. Despite their close relationship, and irrespective of the fact that they had both had been dragged up in Motherwell, the Edinburgh lady had become convinced that living in the capital conferred a degree of social superiority.

'Of course, my dear,' she observed over her skinny latte, 'in this town breeding is everything.'

Her Glaswegian-by-adoption cousin merely lifted one eyebrow and coolly replied, 'Really? Well, we who live in Scotland's metropolis also think it's fun, but we tend to cultivate other interests as well.'

The Hoalidays

DURING THE war my father was an apprentice engineer. At one point he and a friend decided to go for a short holiday to Aberdeen, where the friend had found good digs before with an old Aberdonian lady. One of their fellow apprentices heard them discussing the trip and asked if he might come along. Now, this youth was known as Smudgy, partly because his personal hygiene was the matter of comment and partly because of an accident that had befallen his overcoat. This had been indelibly stained by an incident one night during the blackout. He had been coming home wearing the coat and decided to get a hurl on the back of the 'ghostie', or clenny motor. He jumped onto the vehicle as it passed and, because of the pitch darkness of the night, only in the morning found out that his good coat had been ruined by grease stains. After this he inevitably appeared with it folded over one arm in a gentlemanly manner but was never seen to wear it.

My father and his pal didn't want to offend Smudgy by refusing his company, but when the pair met up at the railway station they were hoping he might have forgotten all about it. Not long before their train was due to depart, Smudgy appeared but, unlike them, he had no suitcase, only a tiny valise.

'Good!' they thought. 'He canny be comin.' But he was. They happened to notice that, uncharacteristically, their chum was wearing a fresh white-collared shirt.

When they got to Aberdeen the old lady assigned them a room with a double and a single bed. Quick as a flash my father and his pal agreed that since Smudgy was the eldest he should have a bed to himself and they claimed the double. An evening walk was decided on and they returned pleasantly tired and ready for sleep. My father and his pal got into their pyjamas and waited for Smudgy to do likewise. After a few minutes he stood up and doffed his jacket and trousers. His 'shirt' quickly fell down over his legs to his knees. It was a long nightshirt! This was the only shirt Smudgy had brought with him, and he wore it throughout their stay in the Granite City, sleeping in it each night.

'He was always well-dressed, Smudgy,' recalled my father. 'He liked to wear a different tie every day to hold up his trousers!'

BUTLIN'S HOLIDAY camp at Ayr has long been a favourite resort for Glaswegians taking their summer holidays in their own country. One fine day at this camp, the punters had enjoyed a display of free-fall parachuting by a detachment of Royal Marines. Afterwards, a football match was arranged between a team from the marines and one from the local Redcoats. A crowd gathered to watch, including Glasgow football fanatics, perhaps suffering close-season withdrawal symptoms. For whatever reason the match became, as the commentators love to say, 'towsy', dirty play soon began to manifest itself and the game degenerated into a highly physical needle-match. Players were going in late, leaving a leg up, taking one another out of the play, and so on.

'There's weans watchin this an aw!' was one of the spectators' shocked observations. Punches now began to be thrown, and eventually a Redcoat had to be stretchered off with an obvious broken leg. At the sight of this, one Glasgow wifie was heard to comment in disgust:

'See whit ye've goat defendin the country? This is the kind of people in the Forces the day!'

SALTCOATS IS another traditional doon-the-watter venue for Glaswegian holidaymakers. When my father was a child, his own father being away at sea, his mother took him and his two brothers to Saltcoats for a holiday. It rained the whole time, but they were still overjoyed when

my father found a ten-bob note in the street (that's 50p to all youse post-decimal punters) because this meant they could stay for another week. It was only when they were on the train back home that the sun at last came out. My grandmother immediately opened the window as far as it would go and urged the boys to sit in the sun so that people would think they'd been away somewhere warm.

A YOUNG Glaswegian was highly disappointed when he went on holiday to the United States. His choice of destination was Nevada, and the problem was that while he had anticipated spending most of his time on the beach, on arriving he found that the state, being landlocked, not only had no beaches, but was nowhere near the sea at all. Cursing, he vowed revenge on the pal back home who had been raving about the Sierra Nevada.

TWO YOUTHS met up in Argyle Street one fine summer day.

'Haw! Check the tan,' said one. 'You been away yer hoalidays?'

'Aye, just back fae two weeks in Greece.'

'Ah'm no long back masel.'

'Couldny've been awful sunny where you were by the look of ye.'

'It wis roastin! Ah wis in Ayia Napa oan wan a they 18–30 shots.'

'Is that right? Must've been 18 oors bevvyin and 30 oors unconscious!'

The Drink

GLASGOW HAS always had a reputation for being a hard-drinking city. It cannot be denied that there is an element of truth in this, but the city is no worse in this respect than many another Scottish community. Where, for example, is a Glaswegian thoroughfare to rival Edinburgh's Rose Street for its sheer number of pubs? What quantities of cheap tonic wine would Glaswegians have to consume to rival the inhabitants of Monklands? You only have to consider, however, the number of terms a Glaswegian can substitute for 'drunk' to recognise that pub society and the recreational use of alcohol play a vivid part in local life. The following anecdotes are loosely hung on this theme, like a drunk onto a lamp-post.

AULD DOOGIE was a wine-mopper. He would broach any vintage as long as it satisfied his two basic requirements of being strong and cheap. Tonic properties were all well and good but not a prerequisite as far as he was concerned. His long-suffering wife had found consolation in the embrace of a new faith and had become a Mormon.

One Saturday afternoon she was entertaining three of the Latter-day Saints to a cup of tea, confident that her husband would be away for most of the day, indulging in his pastime. He was indeed well-away when he put in an unexpected appearance, on the hunt for more drinking money. His wife, black-affronted at his obvious inebriation, sat rooted to her seat, leaving her guests to make their own introductions.

'Good day,' said the first, rising to his feet, 'I'm Elder Johnstone.'

Following suit, the second said, 'I'm Elder Macrae.'

'And I'm Elder Brown,' added the third.

Doogie's bloodshot glance took them all in.

'Pleased tae meet yeez,' he said, 'Ah'm Eldorado.'

ONE HOT summer's day in Glasgow (yes, of course they happen!), an American tourist had wandered off the beaten track on his own, intent on exploring the varied and unusual architecture to be found in little-known parts of the city. After a long spell of walking and photographing, he began to feel the need for some refreshment. Not being entirely sure where he was, he found his guidebook of little use in trying to pinpoint a suitable hostelry, and he settled for the first corner pub he happened upon. It was one of these isolated old-fashioned boozers left standing, like a rock formation in Monument Valley, after the tenement around it has been cleared and demolished. Windowless and drab of exterior, it was less than prepossessing but our visitor was in too much need to be choosy.

He boldly entered; the place was empty but for one or two solitary drinkers and a middle-aged barmaid. The American leaned on the bar, grateful to lay down his heavy bag, and smiled at the barmaid.

'Honey,' he said, as Americans will, 'there's three things I'd like you to give me: something to drink, something to eat, and a few kind words.'

The barmaid tutted derisively and proceeded to pour a pint of Special. She plunked it down on the counter and from a dim recess produced a Scotch pie to accompany it. The Yank surveyed these delights then said:

'Well I see my first two requests, but what about the few kind words?'

Shrugging dismissively the barmaid told him,

'Ah wouldny eat the pie if Ah wis you.'

A YOUNG Ayrshire lad called Ken moved to the big city of Glasgow to study at one of its august universities. As is the way with those engaged in tertiary education these days the youth soon found himself short of money. He was a lad who enjoyed his pint and couldn't help but notice the high cost of beer in the pubs of the metropolis compared to the prices he was used to in his home village. He found he had to restrict his pint intake very carefully as he budgeted his scanty funds and he was always on the lookout for a pub with relatively low prices or extended Happy Hours. One evening he found himself in an out-of the-way little howff where he purchased a pint for what he considered to be a reasonable sum for once and he leant on the bar at his ease, meaning to enjoy this to the full.

As he was drinking a middle-aged man appeared at his side and ordered a pint of heavy. When the barman asked for payment the man handed over the money shaking his head. He turned to Ken and said, 'Some price ye've tae pey fur a jar in here, eh?' Ken was taken by surprise.

'D'ye think so? I thought this place was kind of cheap.'

'Chape? Away ye go, son! Ah'm used tae drinkin in ma club. We would never pit up wi charges lik these.'

By now Ken's interest was truly captured.

'Club, eh? What club's that? Can anybody join?'

The man sipped his beer and frowned.

'It's no a club fur evrubdy, pal. There's some that say we're a bit too coorse an that.'

'Coorse! That'll no bother me, I'm frae Ayrshire! What do you call this club?'

'Well, if ye must know, we call it the Dirty Bastards' Club.'

'Is that right? And how d'you get to be a member?'

'Simple. Ye've just got tae prove tae the Membership Committee that ye are in fact a Dirty Bastard.'

'I reckon I can handle that all right.'

The stranger looked Ken over.

'Tell ye what, then. Ah'll gie ye a chance tae let us see what ye're made of. It so happens that Ah'm on the Committee and Ah've got an application form wi me. You fill this in an ye'll be taken under consideration.'

He finished up his pint and said, 'Right, Ah'm offski. Ah'll be in here same time the morra. Ye can gie us yer form then, right?'

Ken said it was fine with him and thanked him. He took the form home with him to his humble student garret. He filled in the first page with all the usual details and turned over to be confronted with a sheet blank except for the words: *Give details here of why you consider yourself worthy of being recognised as a Dirty Bastard. If necessary, attach a further piece of paper.*

The youth racked his brains all evening, rejecting several exploits as not being gross enough. He was desperate to ensure access to all that cheap beer. What could he possibly put down that would not fail to win him the approval of the Committee? Becoming aware of an imminent bowel movement, he took the form with him to contemplate further as he sat in the toilet. It was then that inspiration struck. He took the blank page and used it to clean his backside. He carefully put the form into an envelope and went to bed triumphant, convinced that with such a stroke of genius he had ensured his success.

Next day he was back at the pub of the day before, and at the same time. Sure enough, the middle-aged man reappeared for a pint of heavy. Ken handed over the sealed envelope with an air of confidence. The man took it, swallowed his beer, and left, promising that they would be in touch.

Over the next few days Ken's assurance began to fade. No mail from the club had arrived. This was taking longer than he had expected. Could something have gone wrong? Eventually he could stand the waiting no longer and made a point of going to the pub where he had first met the Committee man. At the same time as ever the man appeared. Ken greeted him with a slightly offended air but the man was cheerful and brisk and seemed neither up nor down. He was about to finish his drink and go when Ken couldn't restrain his curiosity any further.

'Listen, what happened about my application to join the Dirty Bastards' Club?'

'Oh, did ye no get a letter? The Committee rejected yer application unanimously.'

'But how? I mean, I didn't even write anything on the back page. I just wiped my arse with it! Surely that qualifies me?'

'Naw, naw, son, naw. Don't ye know Dirty Bastards don't wipe their arse?'

A FRIEND of mine was sent by his company, along with a couple of other colleagues from the Glasgow office, on a business trip to Tokyo. He told me how impressive the Japanese operation had been, how their use of computers and their organisation were so much in advance of the Glasgow firm. He and his colleagues had felt 'like country cousins' until, the serious business being concluded, the Japanese hosts invited them for drinks. According to my friend, on such occasions it is a point of honour with Japanese businessmen to get their guests good and drunk. 'How did it go?' I asked. My friend was immediately triumphant.

'We wasted them!' he cried.

I KNOW of a pub whose manager is known to all the regulars as Skipper. Now this is not a title of respect, acknowledging that he is in charge. Neither does it derive from any nautical experience on his part. Rather, the name was earned one night when a crowd of punters were particularly enjoying their evening session and were lingering long past drinking-up time. The manager had asked them to finish up and go several times to no avail, even resorting to an enquiry as to whether or not they had any homes to go to. The drouthy ones considered that their host had become over-importunate to the point of seeming inhospitable. With unspoken agreement the next time he came to chivvy them along, four of them lifted him by a limb each, marched outside and deposited him in something that was handily stationed outside – a skip.

LOTS OF people have been ejected from public houses for

crossing what can be a fine line between behaviour that is acceptable and that which is beyond the pale. Not many, though, can claim to have been flung out of a bar that wasn't open. This distinction was achieved by a friend of mine (let's call him Andy) in the mid-1970s. At this time there was no such thing as all-day opening in the licensed trade. Pubs were obliged to close their doors in the afternoon between the hours of two-thirty and five o'clock. On this particular Saturday Andy and I had been watching a live international from Murrayfield in his flat, regaling ourselves with a few cans of beer. The match having been won, there was nothing for it but to head out for a celebratory pint.

We arrived outside the pub of Andy's choice to find the doors still locked. Andy consulted his watch and showed me that it read five o'clock dead.

'Time this joint was open,' he announced, and began to knock on the door. I suggested trying another establishment, there being plenty to choose from, but Andy's stubborn streak, buoyed up by the beers he had already swallowed, had risen to the top of his consciousness.

'Come on!' he cried to those who must be lurking behind the door but inexplicably ignoring his loud knocking. 'It's gone five an there's punters spittin feathers out here!'

I felt this behaviour was a touch extreme but Andy was deaf to my advice to screw the nut.

'Open up, will ye? Ah'm dyin a thirst!' he yelled, now adding the toe of his boot to the rapping of his knuckles.

At this point we heard the sound of bolts being thrown back and the door opened just enough to expose a grumpy-looking face.

'Thank God for that!' said Andy, attempting to make his way inside. He was halted by a large scarred hand.

'Just haud yer hoarses, you,' advised mine host. 'Ye're barred!' and he quietly reclosed the door.

SOME PEOPLE will go to any lengths to make sure of getting a drink. A Glaswegian tradesman had been working on a government contract on Ascension Island and, the job having come to an end, it was now time to go home. The only mode of transport available to and from this military base was a Royal Air Force flight aboard which no alcohol was allowed. The thought of a long air journey without a wee refreshment was too horrendous a prospect for this particular traveller, and he adopted a wheeze often used by the drouthy at football matches. He got his hands on a syringe and a dozen oranges and injected the fruits with neat vodka. In this way, he passed the long hours of his flight home in contentment. At one point a member of the crew passed by his seat and noticed the bag of oranges and the sucked-dry remains of several already consumed.

'I see you like your fruit,' was his comment.

'Oh aye,' replied the happy wanderer. 'Ah'm a bugger for ma vitamin C.'

IN THE early hours of a Saturday morning a man was walking along the pedestrian precinct in Sauchiehall Street when he spotted a friend coming towards him, obviously the worse for drink. So exaggerated were this person's staggers that he was zig-zagging all over the street, going as far in a sideways direction as in the way he was attempting to progress.

'You're in some state, Davie,' said the man to his drunk friend. 'Where are ye headin anyway?'

'Ah walkin up tae George's Cross,' was the reply.

Fearing that this could take his friend all night at the rate he was proceeding the first man said, 'Why don't ye get a taxi or somethin?'

'Haveny seen wan. Anyway, Ah've nae money.'

'Ah'm rooked masel, or Ah'd gie ye a len a some.'

'S'awright, pal.'

'Well, ye've got a long walk in front a ye, Davie.'

'S'no the length Ah'm botherin aboot . . . it's the breadth!'

IT IS sometimes said that you will find anything and every-thing being sold, unofficially of course, in the pubs of Glasgow. I have certainly been offered some bizarre bargains. One snowy February day I ducked into a Southside bar to dodge a particularly heavy shower. I placed my order and stood wiping snow from my glasses with a handkerchief. When I put the spectacles back on I saw a man standing in front of me.

'Interestit in a perr a specs, pal?' he enquired, holding open a plastic carrier bag half-filled with a variety of frames with lenses in them.

Somewhat surprised, I told him that I didn't need any at the moment.

'Want tae try oan a couple a perr just tae see if they'll dae ye?' the salesman persisted. Again I turned the offer down. He looked a little disappointed, but not upset.

'Ye might slip in that snaw an brek yours,' he said, solic-itously, 'an then where wid ye be?'

I assured him I had a spare pair in the house. He smiled, obviously giving up.

'Just askin, okay, pal?' then went back to his company.

A YOUNG lady at a party was approached by an admirer. He tried out all of his best patter, but to no avail. The object of his desire merely heard him out in silence, a look of scorn straying across her pretty features. As soon as his flow of chat-up lines ground to a halt she sipped at her drink and helpfully suggested:

'Tell ye what, pal. Why don't ye gie it a rest an mibby come back later on. Ah haveny drank enough tae make you interestin yet.'

A CELTIC fan dropped into a pub near Bellahouston Park, scene of the Pope's celebrated visit to Glasgow. As he stood sipping his pint the barman struck up a conversation.

'Aye, we've had all sorts in this boozer, mate. The Pope himself came in for a quick refreshment when he was here.'

The fan was duly impressed and ventured to ask what it was that the Pontiff had quaffed on that occasion.

'It was crème de menthe, as I recall,' said the barman.

'Right,' said the fan, 'if it's good enough for the Holy Father it's good enough for me. Gie's a pint of crème de menthe.'

'A pint? Are ye sure?'

'Why no? Ah'm a pint drinker, amn't Ah? Come ahead.'

The barman shrugged and duly served up this unusual request. The Hoops fan lifted the green pint.

'It's a good colour anyway,' he said as he raised it to his lips. After swallowing a few mouthfuls the fan gasped.

'Man, if that's what he drinks it's no wonder they carry him around in a chair.'

I HAPPENED to be on a bus as it pulled up at a stop in Kilmarnock Road. Last to board the vehicle was a middle-aged man who was quite obviously the worse for drink and was leading a little mongrel. He focused his gaze on the driver, wobbling visibly, and asked him.

'Where are we the now?'

The driver, who had no doubt seen it all before, impassively replied:

'Shawlands, mate.'

The would-be passenger seemed astonished.

'Shawlands!' he cried. 'Aw naw!' He then bent down to speak to his dog:

'D'ye hear that? The man says we're in Shawlands!'

The dog was perfectly calm on receiving this news and hardly raised an eyebrow. The driver meanwhile pulled away from the stop, but if he was expecting to receive a fare what he actually got was another question:

'Hey pal, where is Shawlands, by the way?'

'Southside.'

'Southside? Southside of what?'

'Southside of Glasgow.'

'Southside of Glasgow? How in the name of the Wee Man did we end up here?'

The man then bent to talk to the dog again.

'This is all your fault!' he said.

Like everyone else in earshot I would have loved to hear how the humble canine was to blame, but the next stop was mine.

A MAN stepped into his local and spotted a friend sitting at a table beside another figure, head down amongst the glasses.

'What's the matter wi him?' asked the man.

His friend shrugged, 'Just jaked oot, that's aw. Hell mend him.'

'Are ye annoyed wi him?'

'Ach, he's been windin me up aw night wi his stupit patter. He always talks pure mince when he's bevvied.'

'Just the drink talkin, eh?'

'Aye, I have tae say Ah like the opposite better.'

'What d'ye mean?'

'This: the drink *no* talkin!'

IN A suburban bar Joe and Chaz were having a quiet pint standing at the bar when another man chose to pick a fight with Joe. The latter grabbed his assailant by the arm and threw him over his shoulder to the floor, where he lay stunned.

A stranger said to Chaz, 'Is that kung fu?'

'No way,' says Chaz. 'He's only had the wan pint.'

WEE ALAN was sitting at his favourite corner table in his local pub, just finishing off what would have to be his last pint of the day (owing to the fact that he was now borassic), when a burly bloke rudely flung himself down in a nearby chair, almost upsetting the table and the glass in which Alan's precious last drops of beer were residing. He glared at Alan as if to dare him to make something of it, then took a mouthful of his lager. Alan couldn't help but let his eyes wander to the almost-full pint, covetously noting the bubbles winking at the brim. The surly stranger noted this, then took from his pocket a small pad of yellow sticky notes and a pen. He scribbled something on one of these and fixed it to his tumbler before lurching off to the toilet.

Alan peered at the note and read: 'This pint belongs to the Amateur Heavyweight Boxing Champion of Govanhill.'

When the stranger returned he found his glass was not even half-full. His drink was gone and so was Alan. The label was still on his glass but his original writing had been scored out. Underneath was written a new message, 'This pint is now inside the Amateur Sprint Champion of Pollokshaws.'

The Snappy One-liners

THERE'S A lot to be said for the one-line joke, especially that if they're not helluva funny at least they're over fast.

WHAT DO you call a dwarf that falls into a cement mixer?
  A wee hard man.

WHY WASN'T Jesus born in Glasgow?
  They couldn't find a virgin or three wise men.

WHAT DO you call a guy who takes a small size in a shoe?
  Wee Shooey.

WHAT DO you call a guy that takes a small size in a shoe and can't find his dog?
  Wee Shooey Douglas.

A GUY walks into a GP's surgery.
  'Doctor, doctor!' he cries, 'you've got to help me. I feel like I'm turning into coconut!'
  Says the doctor, 'You're bountae.'

WHAT DID Dracula get when he came to Glasgow?
  A bat in the mouth.

THEN THERE was the guy who went into the carpet trade because he had a flair for it.

THERE WERE three coos in a field. Which wan wis oan its hoalidays?
  The wan wi a wee calf.

WHAT DO you call an illegitimate insect?
  A fly bastart.

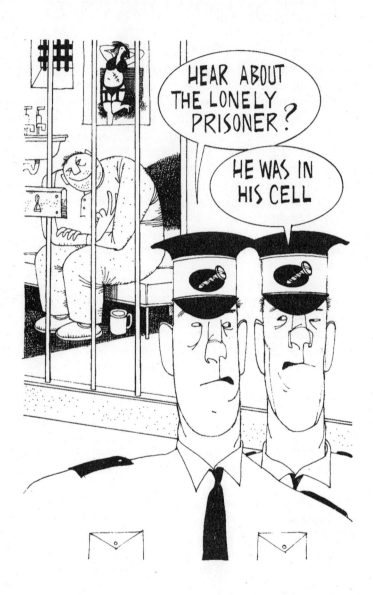

HEAR ABOUT the lonely prisoner?
He was in his cell.

WHAT FAMOUS costume drama TV series of the 1970s was named after a queue for the toilet?
The Aw Needin Line.

HOW IS an old man like a Caramel Wafer?
He's Gray and Dunn.

THE MAN in the clothes shop insisting on a maroon jacket.
'Fur ma roon shooders.'

HEAR ABOUT the stupit skindiver?
He didny have a scuba.

WHERE'S Santa Fe?
The North Pole.

A STONE AGE arrowhead found in Pollok Park has been identified as belonging to a prehistoric Scottish tribe, The Wee Arra People.

HEAR ABOUT the guy whose workmates nicknamed him The Woodpecker? It was because he was always tappin.

DID YOU hear about the London criminal who fell foul of the Glasgow Mafia? Apparently, they made him an offer he couldn't understand.

WHAT'S THE difference between a Rottweiler and a social worker?
Ye can get yer wean back aff a Rottweiler.

HOW MANY Kelvinsiders does it take to change a light bulb?
Two; one to make the gin-and-tonics and one to phone an electrician.

WHAT DO you call a Glaswegian Sikh who enjoys karaoke?
  Gupty Singh.

WHY IS furniture that comes in a flatpack for assembling
by the buyer known as suppository furniture?
  Because ye put it up yersel.

WHAT GOES 'clip-clop, clip-clop, bang! clip-clop, clip-clop'?
  An Eaglesham drive-by.

WHAT DO you call an Egyptian who drives a taxi in
Glasgow? Toot an come oot.

HEAR ABOUT the guy whose nickname was 'Heid Furst'?
His real name was R. Slater.

HEAR ABOUT the taxi driver that took early retirement?
He was fed up with people talking behind his back.

OVERHEARD in a splendid pub in Victoria Road:
  'Just cause this boozer's called 'The Pandora' dizny mean
ye've tae get oot yer box.'

HEAR ABOUT the guy who liked to eat bricks and cement?
  He's awa' noo.'

WHERE CAN you see possums in Glasgow?
  Possumpark.

WHAT DOES a Glaswegian mean if he tells you he's feeling
pony?
  He's a little hoarse.

IF THERE'S nine coos in a field, whit wan's the nearest
tae Iraq?
  Coo eight.

See Glasgow? See Culture?

EVERYBODY KNOWS that Glasgow is hoatching with film companies shooting movies on its mean streets. You can't stroll out for a newspaper without wandering into shot for a thriller or costume drama. Not everybody knows, however, that in a reversal of the Hollywood trend of remaking European movies in versions more suited to a US audience, certain well-known American films are being redone with a Glasgow twist. For example, Coppola's *Apocalypse Now* is being remade as *A Poke a Chips Now*. Similarly, Jonathan Demme's *Silence of the Lambs* is to reappear as *Shut it, Ewes*, and a sequel to Will Smith's sci-fi adventure *I, Robot* is in the pipeline, with the working title, *Naw, Robot*.

A CITY of couch potatoes? Perhaps, but not without a certain native inventiveness. Two friends were talking over a pint about how rotten the telly was. One added:

'As if that wisny enough, the stupit remote control's on the blink.'

'That's nae problem,' said his companion, 'there's this big mate a mines makes them.'

'He makes them? Does he work in a factory or what?'

'Naw, he's on the Aul King Cole, but he says he made a remote for hissel.'

'But how'd he get the bits an aw that?'

'Ah don't know. Look, c'moan we'll take a run up an see him. He can show ye his.'

They finished up their drinks and wandered round to the friend's house. He was ensconced in front of the TV and greeted them amicably when his wife showed them in.

'See how ye told me ye made yer own remote control? Could ye make wan fur ma pal, here?'

'Sure, nae tother.'

'Gauny let us see it, well?'

The inventor demonstated the tool in use. His TV was just the right distance away for its buttons to yield to the pressure of a six-inch nail tied to a garden cane.

'Ah'll run ye up wan the morra,' he said. 'Ye'll need tae supply yer ain nail but.'

IT IS unarguable that Glaswegian authors are in the forefront of current Scottish literature. But as well as those who feature regularly in the short leets for the great literary prizes there are legions of lesser lights toiling away over a hot keyboard. So that they, too, can have their moment of glory, a few of their productions are listed below:

I Was a Streetwalker by Mona Lang

The Martial Arts in Glasgow by Hing Wan Oan

Time to Go by Al O'Way

A Threat of Violence by Ure Dunn

The Art of Diplomacy by Monty Gripps

The Reason Why by Howe Furneaux

Guilty As Charged by Noah Murney and U. R. Sott

Self-Defence for Women by Lisa Lane

Exasperation by C. Euyabamm

Don't Shoot the Banjo-player by Wayne Pluck

What's the News? by Caesar Eckerd

King Solomon's Mine's by the Queen of Sheba

Pardon Me Scratching by Mabozza Ritchie

The Glasgow Diet by Crispin Ginger

TO CONTINUE the theme of writing, there have always been those whose only venture in this field is making out bookies' lines. When my father was young he lived in a close that was painted from ground-level up to a height of about five feet; above that it was whitewashed. One of the neighbours, a man who loved to back a horse and who was short-sighted into the bargain, came into the close to write out a line, leaning on the wall. That task accomplished, he then made his way to his favoured cream cookie. When he handed over his line and cash he was met with a look that was as blank as his betting slip. He had written it all out on the close wall.

HOW DO you spot a Glaswegian intellectual?
    When he chooses 'Delilah' on a karaoke machine it's the Alex Harvey version he prefers.

FIRST YOUTH: 'Ah'll need tae get the granda's telly repaired. He's gaun mental without it. Says it's the only intellectual stimulation he gets, the auld soul.'
    Second youth: 'What's the matter wi it anyway?'
    First youth: 'Ach, he was watchin it the other day an he slung a kick at it.'
    Second youth: 'Whit'd he dae that fur? Did somethin upset him?'
    First youth: 'Aye, he was watchin *Rainbow* an he jumps up an shouts "Ah hate that bastart Zippy! He's always stirrin it!" and puts his boot through the screen.'

DURING THE war, a private in the HLI was making his way back to Maryhill Barracks when the blackout was at its most impenetrable. To add to his difficulties, he had somewhat overindulged in strong waters. At the barracks gate the sentry on duty heard the private's approach without being able to see who was coming.

'Halt!' cried the sentry. 'Who goes there?'

'S'me, Private McGinty,' returned the other soldier.

'Password!' barked the sentry.

'How the hell should Ah know?' was McGinty's indignant reply.

The sentry felt that this was not playing the game.

'Aw c'moan,' he pleaded, 'ye'll need tae dae better than that. How dae Ah know you're no a German paratrooper? Could ye mibby sing us "Scots Wha Hae"?'

'Away! Aw Ah know's the first line!'

'Fair enough! Ye must be a Glesga man at least. In ye come.'

TRIBUTE ACTS have been all the go for a few years. Apparently there is one such band doing the rounds in Glasgow, modelled on the former chart-topping boy-band Take That. It's billed as Take That Ya Bastart.

ONE OF the more iconic images of Glasgow in recent years has been the equestrian statue of the Duke of Wellington in Royal Exchange Square, outside the Gallery of Modern Art, complete with its added adornment of a traffic cone on the great soldier's head. This is taken to exemplify Glaswegian humour, especially in its propensity to deflate the pompous. Photos of the crowned statue have appeared in guidebooks, on postcards and T-shirts so often that the image is famous around the world. While the City Council officially discourages punters from replacing the cone if it ever falls off, there are those who maintain that if the cone does disappear a Council cherry-picker is used to replace it with a new one. Mibbies aye, mibbies naw.

However, the act of citizens interfering with Glasgow's

statues has a longer tradition than you might think. In 1898, the great Scottish writer Neil Munro, perhaps best known for his beloved creation Para Handy, met up with his friend the Polish-born novelist Joseph Conrad, who as a working seaman was in the famously nautical city trying to get a berth on a ship.

After having a drink or two, the authors wandered into George Square, where Munro drew his friend's attention to the statue of James Oswald, MP, which holds in its hand a large lum hat. Munro told Conrad that he could win the status of an honorary Glaswegian if he managed to throw a stone into the hat, and so these two literary giants amused themselves by flinging chuckies at a statue until Conrad managed to perform the feat. Where were the polis?

THE DAY after the famous entertainer Jimmy Logan died, I was in my local newsagent's shop buying my morning paper. Two elderly ladies were being served before me and one of them looked at the front-page headline of her paper and remarked to the newsagent:

'That's shame about Jimmy Logan, isn't it?'

'What about him?' asked the man behind the counter, 'I haven't looked at a paper this morning.'

'He died yesterday, of course.'

'Oh is that right? He must have been a good age. I thought he'd died years ago.'

At this point the second lady spoke up.

'Just watch it . . . he was in my class at school!'

TWO YOUTHS were discussing their favourite kinds of music and one asserted that his current hero was the artist known as Moby.

'Where did he get that name fae anyway?' queried his pal.

'Dunno. Suppose it might be fae *Moby Dick*.'

'What's that then?'

'What are you like? That's a famous fillum wi Gregory Peck an at, ya dobber!'

'Oh aye? Whit's it aboot, VD?'

IT WAS pub-quiz time at a local hostelry, and rivalry was fierce as usual. Two teams were neck-and-neck and everything depended on one final tie-break question:

'In *Star Wars*, who was the son of Obi Wan Kenobi?'

'Ah know this!' cried one excitable punter, 'Obi Two Kenobi!'

SOME SAY that Glasgow has never played a major part in the history of Scotland. It's certainly true that some of its citizens have only a tenuous grasp of the glorious past, and I was reminded of this when a friend reported overhearing this remark in a pub:

'What Scotland needs the day is a great leader. It's time we hud another Wallace the Bruce!'

A GROUP of friends had been to see the Rolling Stones at the SECC. They had all had more than a few drinks both before and during the gig but were gasping for a pint when they came out. Heading back on foot towards the city centre, they were singing and shouting boisterously when they came across the first available pub. Unfortunately for them, there was a bouncer on duty at the door and he obviously didn't like the look of them. The leader of the group decided to remonstrate with the doorman and wouldn't take no for answer. So much did he argue that the bouncer felt obliged to grab him by the lapels with a view to huckling him out of the road. Matters were not improved when one wag in the company decided to address the custodian with the following remark: 'Hey! You! Get affa McLeod!'

Matters Devotional

A SOUTHSIDE priest was about to say Mass one day when he noticed that for some reason the congregation ran to numbers much higher than the usual. He was of course overjoyed to see this, but on making quick mental calculations he realised that the number of Hosts available would never be enough for all the assembled worshippers. Being a quick-thinking individual, the clergyman attracted the attention of a choirboy and whispered into his ear. The youth looked a little surprised but on receipt of an encouraging nod from the priest he sped off to do his bidding. Just in time he returned, somewhat out of breath, and was seen to hand something to the priest. Thus it was that the members of the congregation who were in the latter part of those coming up to take communion found that instead of the standard disc they received a mini-poppadom.

TWO KIDS were talking about religion and its mysteries as relating to the world of adulthood.

'Ma Ma an Da don't go tae church, dae yours?'

'Aye, well ma Ma takes us on a Sunday but ma Da doesny come wi us.'

'How does he get ooty it?'

'Cause he's got his ain religion. It's somethin tae dae wi the Salvation Army an that.'

'How dae ye know?'

'Well, he goes oot at the same time every Saturday night an when he comes hame he's always singin an carryin a copy of the *War Cry*.'

AT A service in an East End chapel the priest surprised everyone by telling the congregation that he was going to take a leaf out of the book of the nearby Barraland traders and sell off from the altar a selection of second-hand items to raise money for charity. He proceeded to list the goods and the prices he might reasonably expect them to go for. He then invited bids. The worshippers were slow to react, being somewhat taken aback by this novel approach to fund-raising, but gradually began to offer sums of cash. When the business was complete the priest invited the lucky bidders to come forward with their money but shocked them all by saying they could forget about taking away the stuff they were paying for. Obviously, he told them, if they were prepared to spend money on these worthless articles they plainly didn't need it as much as the hard-pressed charities, and they could look on their transactions as donations.

A GLASWEGIAN died, and found himself awaking in another place.

'So this is the afterlife?' he thought to himself as he wandered about, taking in his new and strange surroundings.

Eventually he was moved to remark:

'Ah have tae say, Heaven's no much of an improvement on Glasgow.'

At this point a disembodied voice replied:

'What makes you think you're in Heaven?'

A RANGERS fan had died and gone to the big supporters' club in the sky. He had chosen to be cremated, and when in due course his ashes were brought home in an urn the family held a party to mark the occasion. A good few refreshments were had and the old man's favourite party records were played, relatives and friends joining in with gusto and much stamping of feet. At one point during a flute-band number one guest couldn't restrain himself from jumping up and marching about the living room. He staggered close to the fireplace and the hand he reached out to steady himself with almost knocked over the urn containing the honoured remains.

'Careful you!' cried the son of the house. 'That's the ash my father were!'

A PRIEST was paying a pastoral visit to a family who had newly moved into his parish. He got talking with the teenage son of the family and tried to find a mutually interesting topic of conversation.

'Do you like the football?' he asked the youth.

'Oh yes, Father.'

'And what team is it you support?'

'The Celtic, of course!'

'I see . . . and do you often go along to the games?'

'I never miss a game in the whole season. Home or away, I'll be there!'

'Very good. Now, would you consider yourself a good Catholic?'

'Aye, I definitely would.'

'So, do you go to Mass every Sunday?'

'No really, Father . . . I'm no wan of these fanatics or that.'

AT THE Last Supper one of the Apostles was having difficulty finding an unoccupied seat. There seemed to be someone sitting in all of them except for one, where someone had place a bag full of bottles.

'Okay if I sit there?' he asked the company.

'Naw,' came the reply. 'That's fur Judas's kerry-oot.'

Bigotries, Various

THE PUB philosophers were on fine form. It had been a good Saturday night's discussion over just enough drink to promote feelings of kinship and brotherhood with all mankind without tipping over into incoherence and maudlin sentimentality. The unspoken motion had been passed that a man was a man for a' that. The tenor of the evening was somewhat spoiled by the arrival of an interloper who was, shall we say, rather more refreshed than they were and not quite on the wavelength of the mood of the foregoing discussion. He felt obliged to get in his twopenceworth, which was:

'Aye, there's nothin Ah hate worse than bigotry. Except maybe they Orange bastards.'

IT WAS in a supermarket, in the days before apartheid was abolished in South Africa. A lady was examining a display of fine big oranges with an air of uncertainty. A member of staff, setting out more fruit, took the time to ask if he could help in any way.

'Yes,' said the customer, 'maybe you can. I'm trying to find out where these oranges come from but it doesn't seem to be printed on the ticket here.'

The employee had a quick look and was able to state that the fruit in question had been grown in South Africa.

'In that case,' said the lady, 'I'm not buying them.'

'Quite right, hen,' agreed a passing wifie, 'Ah wouldny buy them either. The thought of aw they black hauns on them . . . !'

A MAN walks into a pub carrying a crocodile under one arm. He goes up to the barman and says:

'Hey, mate, do ye serve Tims in this bar?'

One wary eye on the crocodile, the barman replies:

'Aye, sure we do.'

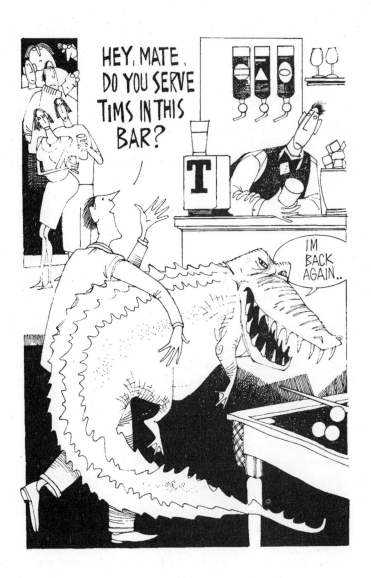

'Okay,' says the customer, 'in that case, a pint of lager for me an a Tim for ma wee pal here.'

THE LONDON-TO-GLASGOW express was making fine time on the last stages of its journey. Just outside Glasgow, however, the passengers were surprised by a sudden series of violent impacts. A concerned traveller made his way to the driver's compartment, where he asked if there was something wrong. The driver reassured him.

'No, it's all right. It was just I had to swerve there because of an Orange Walk.'

'My God! Were they on the line?'

'No they were on the road beside the track.'

A RANGERS supporter is invited to a fancy-dress party and can't think what to go as. He's a bit skint, so he doesn't want to spend a lot of money on hiring a costume. He racks his brains for an idea and just when he's about to chuck it and give the party a bye, he remembers that his late uncle was in the Salvation Army. Maybe his auntie would still have the old guy's uniform and let him borrow it for the night.

He goes round to his auntie's and, sure enough, she's still got her husband's uniform hanging up in a wardrobe. She's not too happy at first about it being used as a fancy-dress costume but she can't refuse her favourite nephew anything for long and eventually agrees as long as he looks after it. He tries it on and (would you believe it?) it's a perfect fit and he takes it away with him.

The night of the party comes and he wanders out with the uniform on. On his way to the bus-stop a heavy shower comes on and, remembering he promised not to get the uniform messed up, he dives into the nearest pub to wait until the rain goes off a bit. The pub's pretty stowed, but he makes his way to the bar and orders a pint. After a mouthful or two of his beer he decides he needs the toilet. So as nobody will think his pint is dead, he sets his hat down on the counter beside it, then heads for the Gents.

When he comes back he discovers that his hat has miraculously filled up with money. There's pound notes, pound coins, and fifty-pence pieces in it right up to the brim. Delighted with his luck, he pockets the dosh, sinks his pint in a couple of gulps and makes for the exit. Just as he reaches the door a voice hails him from the bar:

'Hey, Jim! What about the *War Cry*?'

The Gers fan thinks for a moment then shouts out:

'No surrender!'

TWO FRIENDS were walking down the pedestrianised area of Buchanan Street when they noticed a small crowd assembled in front of a soapbox preacher. Thinking this might afford them a laugh, they went over to hear what the man had to say. The preacher was extolling the joys of being 'born again' and how a new life awaited anyone who underwent this rebirth.

One of the two friends giggled at this point, loudly enough to attract the orator's attention. He fixed the giggler in his steely gaze and, pointing a bony finger at him, said:

'And you, who seem to find salvation a laughing matter . . . would you not welcome the opportunity of being reborn?'

'No way, pal. Ye never know . . . this time Ah might be born a Tim.'

BILLY CONNOLLY tells the story about the late Matt McGinn and himself being confronted by a group of drunken Rangers supporters. The obvious thing was to avoid doing anything to suggest that one was of the Roman Catholic faith. No faintheart, McGinn threw the Bears into such confusion that they simply let the two pass by shouting at them:

'Ya bunch of dirty Orange Fenians!'

A YOUNG man was walking through a suburban street one day when he saw a mad dog attacking a child. Without hesitation he flung himself on the beast, an enormous Rottweiler it was, and pulled it off the terrified infant. The dog was powerful and ferocious and the man had to use so much of his own strength to subdue it that the creature's neck snapped and it died.

Among the small crowd that gathered to help and congratulate the youth was a reporter from the local paper. He told the young man that this would make a wonderful story for his paper and asked for the hero's name and other details. His main hobby, it appeared, was watching football. It occurred to the journalist that this might give him a snappy headline.

'See,' he explained, 'if you were a Falkirk supporter the headline could be "Bairn saves bairn" or if you were a Gers fan it could be "Bear to the rescue" or something like that.'

The youth could appreciate the hack's drift and was happy to tell him that he was a loyal supporter of Celtic. He was not so happy the next day when the local paper printed the story of the event under the headline:

CATHOLIC KILLS FAMILY PET.

A GLASGOW CID man of Afro-Caribbean descent was summoned to take part in halting a disturbance that had broken out at a well-known 'Orange' pub in a suburb of the city. He duly made his way there and entered on a scene reminiscent of a saloon brawl in a John Wayne western. Displaying his warrant card, he shouted to get the combatants' attention. They soon stopped pummelling one another and looked at the stranger in astonishment.

'What's up?' asked the policeman. 'Never come across a Catholic CID man before?'

I HEARD the tale of a couple of Glaswegians who were spending a summer holiday in Spain. They were enjoying a night of serious carousing at a restaurant while staying with Scottish friends in a little Andalucian village somewhat off the usual tourist track. As so often happens, drinking led to singing, and the company belted out all the numbers they knew in common until their fund of songs was exhausted. It was while they were making their somewhat unsteady way home through the village's narrow winding streets that someone had the bright idea of singing 'The Sash'. After all, it was one they all knew, and who could take offence in an out-of-the-way place like this? Certainly not the locals, who would have no idea what it was about. With general agreement they had only just launched into a rousing rendition when a window flew up and from above came another unmistakably Glaswegian voice:

'Gauny shut up, ya shower a Orange bastarts!'

ONE SUNNY July day an alien spacecraft, somewhat off course, happened to land in Glasgow. The pilot, funnily enough a wee green man, stepped outside his craft and looked around. One of the first things to attract his attention was a regular noise of banging and high-pitched musical notes. He made his way towards the source of the sound and found himself confonted by a streetful of people marching together down the street. It being that time of year, the Orange Walk was under way. One of the marchers noticed the stranger and cried out:

'Hey! What are you daein here?'

The extraterrestrial had his translation device switched on and was able both to understand the question and to reply in the same language.

'I'm a Martian,' he said.

The earthman gave a cheery response.

'Well, pal, ye might be the wrang colour but yer heart's in the right place!'

Weans

IN THE bad old days before every flat had its own toilet facilities, children were often afraid to use the stairheid cludgie (communal toilet on a tenement landing) after dark in case The Bogeyman was lurking in it. One such little boy was being quizzed by a new and rather religious primary teacher who essentially wanted to know whether or not the lad was accustomed to saying his prayers before sleep.

'What,' she asked him, 'do you do before you go to bed at night?'

Now this was a smart young fellow and, sure he was on a winner, he brightly replied, 'Ah dae ma hamework, Miss!'

'Very good,' continued the teacher. 'But what I mean is, just before you get into your bed.'

'Brush ma teeth, miss?' offered the child, growing puzzled.

'No, no, no! I mean the very last thing before you go to sleep.'

The boy's face lit up in the certainty of having at last discovered the desired answer.

'Ah pee in the sink, miss!'

IT WAS Christmastime and the music teacher decided a few carols would be nice and seasonal. Hoping to catch the enthusiasm of her class, she asked them to suggest what they might all sing. She nodded to the first wee girl to get her hand up.

'Yes dear?'

'Miss! Can we sing the one about the wean?'

'Well, I'm not really sure which one you mean. Obviously there's a lot of carols about the baby Jesus.'

'Aye, Ah know. But Ah mean the wan that goes on aboot the wean.'

'I'm sorry, child, but I can't think what you mean. A

carol that mentions a "wean"? There's no such thing. Now who else has a suggestion?'

'Oh, but miss! There is!'

Seeing that the girl was in earnest and this wasn't some kind of elaborate mickey-taking exercise, the teacher decided to humour the pupil.

'Oh, very well then. Sing us a verse and we'll see if we all know it.'

In a confident if not entirely tuneful voice the little girl sang:

'A wean in a manager, no crib for a bed,
The little lord Jesus laid down his wee head . . .'

A LITTLE boy was taken to task by his mother who had found cigarettes in the pockets of a pair of trousers she was about to wash.

'So you're smokin, are ye? Ah thought ye had more sense. We'll soon put a stop to this carry-on, though.'

'But Mum, it's all right to smoke. It must be, because Jesus smokes.'

'Ya cheeky wee monkey! What are ye talkin about?'

'Well, didn't the minister say we've to bring all our dowts to Jesus?'

AN UNEMPLOYED man supplemented his meagre income by collecting bits and pieces of scrap metal and selling them to a dealer. On one occasion he had gathered a fair amount of the stuff and was awaiting the weekly visit of the local rag and bone man. Before the dealer had appeared one of the man's friends called round to ask him out for a pint. He accepted and told his wife to wait in for the rag and bone man and be sure to get a good price for the scrap he had put so much effort into amassing. The wife was happy enough to do this but as the afternoon wore on she became impatient. She didn't see why she should have to be stuck indoors on a perfectly good day. Finally, she decided enough was enough and went out herself,

THE SINK ▲

◀ STAIR
HEID
CLUDGIE

telling her daughter, who was playing in the garden with her pals, to look after the scrap until the man came for it. In due time her husband returned home, cheery with the couple of pints he'd had and the thought of the ready cash he had been waiting for finally being at his disposal.

He met his daughter playing at the gate, blowing loudly on a toy whistle.

'Hi, hen,' he greeted her. 'Where'd ye get the whistle?'

'The nice man that took away the scrap gave us it.'

A wave of fear swept over the child's father and his face turned pale.

'That wouldny be aw he gied ye, wouldn't it no?'

'Of course no, daddy . . .' said the girl.

The man sighed with relief, then his daughter went on: 'He gied us a balloon as well but it blew away.'

TWO YOUNG mothers were comparing notes about their respective toddlers. The first one said:

'The wean gave us an awful fright the other day.'

'How, whit happened?'

'Ah went oot tae the kitchen fur a wee minute an when Ah came back in he wis eatin a comic!'

'Eatin a comic? Did he swally any of it?'

'Aye, a great big chunk.'

'But wis he awright?'

'Aye, Ah just pattit his back till he fartit a beezer.'

Know What Ah'm Sayin?

GLASGOW IS well known for having a language of its own (someone should write a book about it) and this can sometimes lead to misunderstandings in conversation. The following are a few examples of what happens when someone thinks what you meant wasn't what you said, or something like that.

A SCHOOLTEACHER, not native to Glasgow, is getting to know her class on the first day of the new school year. Her method is to try to draw information from her charges by encouraging them to describe their own neighbourhood and say what they think about it. Having established the whereabouts of one child's home, she turns to the next boy.

'And do you live in the same street?' she enquires.

'Naw,' says the youth, somewhat dismissively, 'Ah stey in a boat hoose.'

'Really? That's very interesting and surely quite unusual. Tell me, where is it moored?'

'Whit?'

'Well, I mean is it kept on a river, or perhaps on a canal?'

'Eh? It's jist in a road.'

'In a road? But didn't you say it was a boat house?'

'Course Ah did. The cooncil were sellin it an ma Da boat it.'

TWO MATURE ladies were sitting on a park bench in the afternoon sun when they spied a young couple coming towards them. One said:

'Here Nettie, isn't that your Liz comin?'

'Aye, that's her an her new boyfriend.'

The first lady looked a little puzzled but had no time to speak further before the newcomers were halting in front of them. Introductions were made and small talk exchanged before the young pair went on their way.

'He's a nice young lad, that,' said Nettie.

'Aye, he's that polite,' said her friend, who then added, 'Ah fair got a surprise when Ah saw he wis white.'

'What?' asked Nettie, taken by surprise. 'What made ye think he wisny?'

'Well, did you no say he was a keen yin?'

ON THE day her exam results were issued, a student was phoning her mother to pass on the good news.

'Ah've passed them aw, Mammy!'

'Good for you, hen. Ah knew ye had it in ye!'

'It's not only that, though. Ah'm gettin "Merit" as well!'

'Whit? We'll see aboot that, ma girl! Efter me an yer Daddy scrimpin an savin tae pit you through that college? There no way you're gettin merit till ye've brought some money inty this hoose!'

MANY YEARS ago, a loving husband was deeply saddened by the death of his wife. When it came to the necessary business of ordering a gravestone, he thought long and hard about a suitable inscription. Being a religious man, he decided a scriptural quotation would be best and from his Bible he selected the proverb:

'A virtuous woman is a crown to her husband.'

In due course a stonemason came to be at work on the gravestone in question. Having inscribed the usual details of name and dates, he began on the quotation. Before he was far into it he realised that there would not be enough space to record the whole sentence. He put down his tools and upbraided himself for his lack of foresight. If only the message could be shortened in some way without losing its sense. Inspiration struck and he eagerly went back to work. It was greatly to the mourning husband's consternation when, on his first sight of the finished stone, he read:

'A virtuous woman is 5/ - to her husband.'

I WALKED into a newsagent early one morning and sleepily requested a newspaper.

'*Herald*, please.'

From the massed ranks of sweeties in front of him the newsagent unhesitatingly plucked and deposited before me: an Aero.

(It is necessary for appreciating this one to grasp that in broad Glaswegian pronunciation Aero comes out as 'Erro'.)

THE SHORT-SIGHTED lady in the baker's shop was peering at the display of cakes under glass.

'Tell me, dear,' she asked the girl at the counter, pointing at one confection in particular, 'I've come out without my glasses. Is that a doughnut or a meringue?'

'Naw, ye're absolutely right, missis. It's a doughnut okay.'

AN ART teacher was imparting to her charges the skills of making collages out of various materials. It occurred to her that the last time she had looked in the Art room's large walk-in cupboard she had noticed a roll of felt that would come in handy for just this exercise. She wasn't sure if there was enough for all her pupils and entered the cupboard to check. She failed to understand the howls of laughter, especially from the boys, that greeted her innocent remark:

'Now, follow me into the cupboard anyone who wants felt.'

IT WAS Folk Night at the local bar. An enthusiastic youth with a guitar was battering out an old Australian sheep-shearer's song. When he came to a line about having to 'shear a tally' before the end of the day's work, one punter turned to another and enquired:

'What is it he's got against Italians anyway?'

A STORY from the nineteenth century is told of a countryman who wanted to visit a relation who had been
confined to Gartnavel Lunatic Asylum. He enlisted the
help of his minister, who knew Glasgow well, to take
him to the place. Passing through the city, the minister
took it into his head to look into the city Exchange to
greet a friend. Distractedly, he neglected to tell his parish-
ioner of this detour. The countryman saw the inhabitants of the Exchange excitedly crossing and recrossing
the floor and conducting shouted conversations. He
ducked behind the minister with an alarmed look on
his face.

'What's the matter with ye, man?' asked the clergyman,
puzzled.

'Is it safe, minister?'

'What do you mean, is it safe?'

'Well, they're aw runnin aboot lowse!'

SEVERAL CRONIES were in the bookie's discussing the
day's bankers and bingers. One said:

'A big mate a mine's gied us a great wee tip. Says it's a
cert.'

'Oh aye, what is it?'

'That's ma problem ... Ah canny mind the hoarse's
name. It's bound tae win, but. It's a nice-looking big animal
wi a white star oan its face.'

'That's no criterion!'

'Naw, that wasny its name. Ah'll get it yet!'

MRS DUNN, a Glasgow mother, was worried about her
son. He had left home a few weeks ago to seek his fame
and fortune in the gold-paved city of London and, apart
from a phone call on his first night there to let her know
he had made it down safely, she had heard nothing from
him. She learned from a neighbour that another young
man from the area was soon leaving for the same desti-

nation and she went round to his house to have a word with him.

'See when ye're doon there in London? Could ye mibby have a look fur ma boay Neilly? He promised tae write every week an Ah've no had a letter fae um yet.'

The youth, though not of the brightest, was willing to help, but he had his doubts:

'Ah'll dae ma best tae get a haud ae um, missis, but London's a big place, ye know.'

'It canny be that big, son. Ah'm sure ye'll find um if ye try.'

The young man agreed to try his hardest. When he arrived at Euston Station he found that his most pressing need was to find a toilet. To his dismay he discovered that the facilities were in great demand and he was unable immediately to secure the necessary cubicle. He lingered outside the first one until desperation forced him to knock on its door.

'Are you writin yer memoirs in there or what?' he demanded.

He was surprised to hear the accent of a fellow Glaswegian issue from within:

'Hing oan a wee minute, pal. Ah'm neally done, but there's nae paper.'

'Oh? Is that why ye huvny wrote tae yer mammy?'

THE AMERICAN writer Maya Angelou gave a reading in a local bookshop, followed by a signing session. She had told the audience about some of the trials of her life that she had used as the raw material for her work, including having been raped as a child and struggling against discrimination and poverty to bring up her son on her own. This was on the mind of one reader who, while waiting for the author to sign a copy of her latest book, sympathetically said:

'Aye, ye've had a bad hurl, right enough, hen.'

The American, puzzled, wondered why anyone thought she had been sick.

A FRIEND of mine was on his way out to the shops to gather the necessaries for a meal he and his wife were entertaining another couple to that evening when his wife called after him to remember to buy some incense sticks. Having completed the bulk of the purchases, he entered a likely-looking shop with this final errand in mind.

'Got any joss-sticks, captain?' he enquired of the shop-keeper.

'Aye, no problem,' was the reply. 'What kind are ye after?'

'Got sandalwood?'

The shopkeeper scratched his head.

'Sandalwood? Ah'm no sure, pal. Wait a wee minute till Ah have a look.'

He bent under the counter and began to take out cardboard boxes bearing brand names like Sony and Amiga and Sega. Having rooted around for a good few minutes, he stuck his head up and asked:

'Sorry, pal . . . what kinna computer is it ye've got?'

I WAS told the story of a young mother whose children were treating her to a particularly harassing day. She was trying to referee their fights, meet their demands for sustenance and amusement, and at the same time make conversation with an elderly lady neighbour, rather hard of hearing, who had dropped in for a cup of tea and a blether. The younger woman complained of being driven mad by her children:

'If this carries on I'm going to end up in a straitjacket!'

Obviously hearing this as something about a new jacket, the old lady smiled and said:

'Ah wish ye health tae wear it!'

I WAS having a drink with a couple of friends when the conversation turned to the subject of holidays. One of my companions had recently returned from France and was enthusiastic in its praise.

'What part of France were ye in?' enquired my other pal.

'Brittany,' was the reply.

'Is that right? I was in Brittany a couple of years ago.'

'Oh aye? Quimper?'

'Naw, bed an breakfast.'

(Readers unfamiliar with the pronunciation of 'Quimper' should note that it is 'kam-perr'.)

IT WAS a young lad's first day as an apprentice painter in a Govan shipyard. He was issued with his brushes and other gear and taken by a foreman to meet the man he would be working under, who was busily painting away. The foreman introduced them, then left them alone.

'Okay, son,' said the time-served man, 'gauny see us that wid?'

The youth looked about his feet for the piece of wood in question but couldn't see any.

'Whit d'ye mean?' he said.

'That wid,' said the man. 'Gie's that wid!'

'But Ah canny see any. Where is it?'

'Son, if Ah don't get that wid an get it oan this tin ma paint's gauny dwy up!'

A LOCAL radio station was taking part in a fund-raising drive for charity and invited listeners to phone in with offers of unwanted possessions that could be auctioned to raise money for the good cause. The DJ was delighted when one frail-sounding old lady called to offer a piano.

'Somebody else would be as well havin it, son. Ah canny play a note. It's jist collectin dust.'

'That's very generous of you. But does nobody else in the house play?'

'Ma man used to play a bit but he passed away a few years ago . . .'

'Sorry to hear that . . .'

'Ach well, such is life. Now, ma boay . . . he wis a great

wee player, but he stays in England now. It's jist me in the hoose masel.'

'It's awful good of you, missus. Could we just get some details about the piano from you?'

'Whit d'ye mean, son?'

'Well, is it a grand piano?'

'Grand? It's a f***in stoater!'

A SOUTHSIDE couple had come to the age when both were retiring from work. With their children having fled the nest, they now reckoned that the family home was too big for them and decided to move to a nice wee bungalow in Crossmyloof. Before departing, they made a point of telling their postman, with whom they had become on very friendly terms over the years.

'Oh, that'll be a lovely place tae stay,' he enthused.

'Aye,' said the husband, 'we've had oor eye on it for a wee while.' His wife agreed, 'It's a thought to leave the old place but we're fair lookin forward to movin.'

'One thing's a cert,' said the postie, 'ye'll definitely be sure tae get the weather over there.'

'The weather?' asked the man, plainly puzzled.

'Aye, the sun's always shinin there, intit?'

'What, in Crossmyloof?'

'Oh *Crossmyloof!* Ah thought ye said Magaluf!'

I ONCE knew a French student who, as part of her university course qualifying her to become an English teacher, came to work in a Glasgow secondary school as a French assistant. Her English was already excellent, but she found a certain amount of difficulty in following the speech of her pupils and the citizens she met in daily life. She gradually adapted to the Glasgow accent, but she told me this story about a misunderstanding that happened not long after she had first moved into her tenement flat in the West End.

She shared a landing with an elderly widow, Mrs Niven,

who was always friendly and helpful and keen to draw her into conversation. One autumn day, on which the first chill of approaching winter had made itself felt, the French girl was heading up the close stairs after a hard day at the chalkface when she encountered her neighbour on the way down.

'Hello, hen!' greeted Mrs Niven. 'Wee bittie cauld the day!'

'I'm sorry,' replied the student, 'what did you say?'

'Ah says "Wee bittie cauld the day."'

The French girl was totally puzzled, but hated the thought of offending her neighbour by asking her to repeat herself yet again. So she gave it her best shot:

'I'm sorry, Mrs Niven, but I don't know who Wee Betty is or why she has called me.'

A GLASWEGIAN businessman, in the course of some entrepreneurial mission, found himself obliged to spend the night in Manchester. He sought out a hotel that looked as if it might be reasonably priced and proceeded to check in.

The desk clerk, on hearing the new guest's Scottish accent, and no doubt wishing to relieve the boredom by having a little fun at the stranger's expense, was moved to enquire:

'Would sir like The Tartan Room?'

Clearly unamused by such banter, the Glasgow man replied:

'No, just the room'll be fine.'

ON A similar note, the tale is told of an elderly Glaswegian who, having strayed unknowingly into an area of the city where ladies of the night ply their trade, was accosted by one of them who asked if he would like 'Supersex'.

A little puzzled, the man thought a moment before replying:

'Oh I don't know . . . what kinna soup is it?'

A GLASWEGIAN hailed a taxi in Victoria Road, climbed in and asked the driver to drop him in Hope Street. The driver turned to his passenger and in a heavily accented voice asked him to repeat what he had said.

'My English, she not so good,' he explained.

The passenger asked for Hope Street once more, taking care to speak slowly and clearly. The driver nodded in understanding this time and the passenger couldn't help but notice that he was wearing a strange hat made out of fur. It looked like the kind of thing Daniel Boone or Davy Crockett sported in movies but in this case it seemed to made from the pelt of a fox rather than a raccoon.

'You not from around here, eh pal?' he observed.

'No, my friend,' replied the driver, 'I am from Poland. I am accountant, but make more money driving taxi here.'

'Oh aye? Very good. D'ye like livin in Glasgow then?'

'Very very nice. People very friendly. Always want to talk to me when they find out I am a foreign.'

'Aye, they're no bad that way,' agreed the Glaswegian, always keen to maintain the good name of his home town. He couldn't help but keep looking at the hack driver's headgear, the white-tipped tail of which was waving around as its owner spoke. Eventually he just had to ask.

'Eh, by the way, mate . . . what's the story of the furry bunnit?'

'The what? Oh this hat? Everybody tell me to wear it when I first come to Scotland, so I think it must be custom.'

'Ah don't get ye.'

The driver shrugged.

'When I first come here, many people say to me "Where you come from?" and when I tell them "Gdansk", they all say same thing: "Wear the fox hat."'

A PASSENGER plane from Prestwick to Florida was in the air midway over the Atlantic when it suddenly found itself in trouble. The pilot made an announcement to the effect that, while no-one should panic, all the engines had simultaneously failed, leaving them with no option but to crash-land in the sea, an event which few if any of them would be likely to survive.

After the initial outburst of terror and despair from the passengers, an attractive young woman leapt to her feet, ripped off her blouse and cried out in an impassioned, urgent voice,

'Will somebody make me feel like a woman for the last time?!!'

A few seats behind a man sprang up, pulled his shirt over his head, and with equal fervour replied,

'Nae problem, hen! Here, iron this!'

The Gemme

WHILE IT is true that the sports played in Glasgow are many and various (ferret-racing on the banks of the Forth and Clyde Canal springs instantaneously to mind), it cannot be denied that the most popular of these with both participants and onlookers must be football. Furthermore, to the majority of soccer aficionados outwith the legions faithful to Partick Thistle, Queen's Park, or maybe even Pollok Juniors, Glasgow football is synonymous with the eternal rivalry of Rangers and Celtic. Old Firm humour is a rich and heady brew, often over-powerful for those with tender susceptibilities, and no prisoners are taken by either side. Such samples as are contained in this chapter represent what I consider the least offensive among the current vintage in circulation. It of course behoves a disinterested writer to be strictly non-partisan in this field, so I've tried to be as rotten to one side as the other.

THE STORY is told of Danny McGrain, who never let the fact that he suffered from diabetes hold him back from attaining many of the game's honours with both Celtic and Scotland, playing in an international at Hampden. As is often the case when the Scottish lads are not particularly setting the heather on fire, a section of the home support had divided along Old Firm lines to barrack players earning regular wages for the team they respectively loved to hate. From the Rangers end one Bluenose yelled:

'See you, McGrain? Ye're a useless Tim bastard!'

A fan in the row behind was moved to comment.

'That's you showin yer ignorance, pal. It's well known McGrain's a Protestant.'

'Is that a fact? Hey, McGrain! Ye're a useless diabetic bastard!'

A CELTIC fan was on his way out to a midweek match when his wife accosted him at the front door.

'Is this you away tae another gemme?'

'Aye, what of it?'

'Well, is wance a week no enough fur ye?'

'Gie's peace, wummin,' said the fan, carelessly wrapping his green-and-white scarf around his neck, 'Ah'm only gaun tae the fitba.'

'See you an yer stupit fitba? Whit aboot me? Ye never think tae take me oot. Sometimes Ah reckon ye think mair of the Celtic than ye do of me.'

'Listen hen, Ah think mair of the RANGERS than Ah do of you!'

TWO CELTIC supporters were sitting in their local one Saturday afternoon watching the news on television while waiting for the classified results to come up. One got up to go and get the next round in. When he came back he was surprised to discover his pal gazing fixedly at the screen with tears in his eyes.

'What's the matter wi you?' he enquired.

'It was this item on the news,' the other Bhoy explained. 'They said a Rangers supporters' bus was in a smash on the motorway. It somersaulted three times, ended up on its roof, and everybody in it wis kilt.'

'That's terrible, so it is. But hey, you're getting awful soft-hearted, aren't ye no? I've seen a time when you'd've been laughin at that, no greetin.'

'Well, the worst of it is,' said his pal, wiping away a tear in a rough manly way, 'there were three empty seats on that bus.'

AT AN Old Firm Cup Final the swelling throng of supporters eager to get into the ground was being kept in check by mounted police, among their ranks a female officer. One truculent fan took exception to being nudged by the WPC's steed.

AN HISTORIC MOMENT....

'Haw! Gauny watch who ye're shovin wi that daft hoarse? It's lashin wi sweat!'

The policewoman, having seen and heard it all before, boredly replied:

'Aye, an you'd be lashin wi sweat if it wis you between ma legs. Now move!'

A WELL-KNOWN extortion racket is operated outside football grounds on match days by opportunistic and entrepreneurial wee boys who offer to 'watch your car' for a fee. Implied in the offer is the threat that damage to the vehicle may originate with those denied the opportunity of supplying the service. On one such occasion a fan was parking in the street close to Firhill when some tiny youths made the traditional approach.

'Watch yer car fur ye, mister?'

The Jags fan turned the boys down, pointing to the large Doberman glaring from the back seat, looking as if he considered children a playpiece.

'Ah don't need any help tae mind ma motor wi Killer in it,' he boasted.

On his return to his car after the game (and being a Thistle supporter he no doubt already lacked reason to celebrate) he found that all of his tyres were flat. A closer look revealed a rough note scrawled on a piece of litter tucked beneath his windscreen wiper. To his chagrin, he read:

'If Kilur is so brilyent get him to blaw up yoor tires.'

OLD FIRM supporters are nothing if not widely travelled and they have a tendency to turn up in the farthest-flung corners of the world, even (believe it or not) in places where they don't play football. The story is told of a merchant ship off the coast of Australia which was summoned by radio to go to the rescue of an airliner that had been forced to ditch in the sea. When the ship arrived at the scene the crew were horrified to find that every one of the unfortunate passengers had been eaten by sharks. All, that is, except one wee man seen floating in the water clinging to a piece of wreckage. He was thrown a line and duly hoisted aboard, where he lay on the deck exhausted, clad in only his underpants. The captain looked on as his medical officer attended to the half-conscious survivor.

'Now that's what I call a lucky man,' he said. 'I wonder what quirk of fate decided that he would be the only one to live.'

His first mate, a Govan man, was quick to come up with the answer.

'That's easy. See that tattoo on his chest?'

The captain stooped to examine the tattoo.

'What does it say? Glasgow Celtic, best in Europe.'

The first mate shrugged. 'There ye are. No even a shark wid swallow that.'

ONE DAY at Jamaica Street Bridge a man was seen to climb onto the parapet claiming that he had reached the end of his tether and was going to end it all. From the crowd that quickly formed a Good Samaritan stepped forward to try to talk the poor fellow out of it.

'I'm sure you think life looks pretty bleak at the moment,' he said, 'but spare a thought for your family before you do anything rash.'

'Ah haveny got any family,' muttered he-who-would-be-not-long-for-this-world.

The lifesaver thought for a moment then tried another approach.

'Well, what about your football team? Aren't they some-thing to live for? Think about the good old Rangers!'

'Ah don't support the Gers.'

'The Celtic then; think about the grand old Celts.'

'Ah don't support them either.'

'In that case,' observed the do-gooder in obvious disgust, 'ye might as well jump, ya atheistic get, ye.'

THE STORY is told (and as with many alleged true stories only the people involved can actually verify it) of Celtic's Bobby Lennox and Rangers' Derek Johnstone finding themselves on the same players' bus as members of a Scotland international team on the way home from a match back in the 1970s. The lads were in jovial mood (perhaps they had actually won) and were amusing themselves by singing a few songs. Johnstone mischievously asked Lennox to sing 'The Sash' just for fun. Lennox took this in good part but declined. Johnstone was determined, however, and kept repeating his request until the Celtic player finally gave in and agreed to give it a go.

'It is old and it is beautiful . . .' he began, and then stopped.

'What about the rest of it?' said Johnstone.

'Sorry,' Lennox apologised, 'I don't know any more of it.'

'What do you mean, you don't know the rest of it?' cried the Rangers man, astonished. 'You must have heard it loads of times at Old Firm games.'

'Sure, but I've never heard the rest of it.'

'How can that possibly be?'

'Well, we usually score at that point.'

WHAT IS it that Rangers, Celtic, and a three-pin plug have in common?

They're all completely useless in Europe.

SOMETIMES WHEN your team is going through a prolonged slump in form, even the most diehard of fans can find it a bit hard to bear. During one of Celtic's bad spells, the mother of a young teenager saw in the local paper that the Bhoys had just released a new jersey design. Knowing that her son had supported the Parkhead side through good fortune and bad, and aware that his birthday was coming up, she handed him the necessary sum of money and told him to go and buy himself the new strip.

'No,' he said, 'it's okay, Mum. I'm not that bothered about it.'

'Come on,' she insisted, 'you've been a good boy, stickin in at school and all that. You deserve it, son. Off ye go.'

Still with a show of reluctance, the youth gave in and agreed to go into town to seek out the gear. When he came back from his shopping trip he closed the front door behind him and went straight to his room. His mother, expecting to be shown the new purchase, puzzledly followed him. There on his bed was an assortment of dirty books, an inflatable woman and several packets of condoms.

'What the blazes is this?' the mother demanded, horrified.

Shamefacedly, the boy replied, 'I'm sorry, Mum; I tried really hard but I'm just too embarrassed to go into a shop and ask for a Celtic strip.'

IT IS a little-known fact that certain of the popular chants heard at Old Firm games are not only a lot older than might be expected but actually have their origins in antiquity. By way of illustration, consider Attila the Hun. In his all-conquering sweep across fifth-century Europe (he could always count on a substantial travelling support) he arrived before the gates of Rome and demanded the city's surrender. The pope of the day gave him short shrift and his defiant words echo from the pages of history to this day: 'Go home, ya Hun!'

Attila, undaunted by any authority, whether temporal or spiritual, gave an even more succinct reply which is robustly commemorated at the end of many a cheery anthem sung by the Ibrox faithful.

NOT UNCONNECTED with the above is the story told of a Celtic supporters' social club with a bar manageress who not only tolerates no nonsense but is a Protestant to boot. This is why she is known as The Hun at the Till.

A CONSIDERABLE stramash, as they like to say in foot-balling circles, was created when Maurice 'Mo' Johnstone performed the rare feat of playing for both sides of the Old Firm. What was particularly unforgivable to the Parkhead faithful was the fact that Johnstone had seemed to be on the verge of agreeing terms for a return to Parkhead when he had suddenly switched his allegiance to Rangers. The story was told around this time that a daughter of a Celtic-supporting family had given birth to quadruplets and, being stuck for names, had called them Eeny, Meeny, Miney, and . . . Jimmy.

IT WAS half-time at an Old Firm game. In the dressing room a Protestant player recently signed by Celtic was complaining to one of his new team-mates that he was having something of a hard time keeping his mind on the game.

'What's the problem?' his colleague enquired.

'Well, it's just there's something bothering me.'

'What's that?'

'See when I ran out on the park? I could hear Rangers fans calling me a Fenian bastard.'

'Ach, don't pay any mind to that. You'll soon get used to it and then it'll be water off a duck's back.'

The new Celt was not, however, mollified.

'It's all right for you,' he said. 'You *are* one.'

WHEN THE former Argentinian international player Ossie Ardiles was manager of Swindon Town, his club was punished by the football authorities for certain illicit goings-on by being demoted by two divisions of the league. In a Glasgow pub two punters were watching this story being broadcast on the TV news when one turned to the other and observed,

'The last time Ah saw an Argentinian goin doon two leagues that fast he wis the captain of the *Belgrano*.'

AT A time when there seemed to be a rash of highly-publicised scandals about Catholic priests not living up to their vows of celibacy and even fathering children, the joke went round that Celtic had boosted attendance at Parkhead by introducing a special new gate for 'Priests and sons'.

AT IBROX one Saturday afternoon two Rangers supporters were seated side by side. One had his transistor radio glued to his ear, following the live commentary from Celtic Park, as desperate to learn how badly the Enemy were doing as he was to take in the action of the game in front of him. At one point he couldn't restrain a groan.

'What's up?' his pal asked.

'The ref's went an gied the Tims a penalty.'

'Away!' cried the other Bear. 'That wis never a penalty!'

THE RANGERS Board of Directors decided to hold a competition to find the club's most loyal supporter. Entries flooded in from all over the country as well as from the far-flung Bears supporters' clubs throughout the world. It was a long and difficult task to pick the winner but this was eventually accomplished. The lucky fan turned out to be an 80-year-old Govan man who had followed the Gers, man and boy, since he was five years old. He was treated to an all-expenses-paid day as the club's guest, visiting the trophy room and dressing rooms. He then enjoyed a slap-up pre-match lunch before being taken on the team bus to an away game at Hibs, where he watched the play from the directors' box. The team duly obliged with a convincing win and the elderly fan enjoyed the celebrations on the team bus back to Ibrox.

At the end of a lavish dinner the chairman made a short speech of thanks to the supporter for his long devotion to his club, winding up by asking him if there was any particular season in Rangers' history that he had enjoyed more than others. The old Govanite gave it some thought and wasn't long in coming up with an answer:

'That would be 1977–78.'

The chairman's memory failed him in trying to sum up the club's achievements at that era.

'Was that the year we won the treble?' he asked.

'No, no,' said the fan, 'that was the year two popes died and Danny McGrain had a broken leg.'

ONE SATURDAY a Rangers fan went to an Old Firm game at Parkhead. Arriving a little late, he got a bit flustered and in his rush went into the Celtic end by mistake. By the time he realised his blunder the match had already kicked off. Not wishing to miss a moment of the action, he shrugged and sat down. It wasn't long before a Celtic fan sitting next to him spotted his Rangers scarf.

'You better keep your mouth shut, pal,' he was warned, 'or you're on a doing.'

The Gers fan tried to keep his enthusiasm under control but when his team scored in the fifteenth minute he couldn't help jumping to his feet in joy. He was quickly huckled back down by a Celts fan on each side and reminded to behave himself, or else.

As fate would have it, Rangers scored again just on the stroke of half-time and the Bear managed to stay in his seat but couldn't restrain a cry of 'Yes!' The surrounding Bhoys glared at him and one big bruiser jabbed him with his finger.

'Right you, that's half-time. Away and get me a Bovril.'

The Rangers man thought this was his chance to escape to a more friendly part of the ground and agreed to do what he was told. But before he could move the Celts fan ordered him to hand over his left shoe as a guarantee that he would come back. In dismay the Gers fan handed over his shoe and hopped off on his errand. When he returned the Celts fan took the Bovril, pointed at the shoe on the floor and commanded him to put it on. He did so and his foot immediately came in contact with something soft and with a sickeningly unmistakable odour.

'Oh shit,' he cried.

The surrounding Junglies laughed and he thought he might be spared further humiliation and be able to escape, but his tormentor wasn't finished.

'Right, give me your other shoe while you go and get a Bovril for my pal here.'

The fan had no choice and once more hopped away, this time with a squelch. He had a good idea what would be waiting for him when he came back and, sure enough, his right foot had to squeeze in beside another malodorous lump. He was allowed to sit out the rest of the match in peace, albeit smelly and highly uncomfortable, and even though Rangers ran out winners he didn't feel much like celebrating.

As he left the ground a radio reporter came up to him eagerly.

'Unless I'm mistaken,' said the hack, 'this is a Rangers supporter coming out of the Celtic end. Can I ask you, sir, does this signal an end to the trouble at Old Firm games?'

The fan shook his head.

'No, I can't say it does. I think there's always going to be bother at these matches.'

'What makes you so sure of that?'

'Well, put it this way. As long as they keep crapping in our shoes we'll keep peeing in their Bovril,' he told the puzzled reporter and wandered away.

A RANGERS fan wanders into a pub with his dog to watch his idols perform in a televised live match. He stands at the bar and his dog lies at his feet, also watching the TV screen. It's not the Gers' day and the Boys in Blue lose the match. As the final whistle goes and the commentator reads out the score, the dog starts barking wildly, leaping up and down, and biting lumps out of the leg of the nearest bar stool. The barman watches this in astonishment, then asks the Rangers fan:

'Here, what's got inty your dug?'

The fan shrugs resignedly and replies:

'Well, he's Rangers-daft, that dug. He really does his nut when they get beat.'

'Is that a fact?' says the barman. 'And what does he get up to when they win?'

'I don't know,' says the Rangers fan. 'I've only had him the six months.'

A FEW years back, the Rangers keeper Andy Goram withdrew from a midweek international game on the grounds that he was not mentally prepared for it. In no time, as is always the way, rumours soon spread that he was seeking psychiatric help in that department. The next time he turned out for his club a section of the opposition support began to chant: 'Two Andy Gorams . . . There's only two Andy Gorams.'

A GAME at Firhill was not going the Jags' way and there were few thrills for the home support. Late in the second half one of the Maryhill Magyars was knocked unconscious in a clash of heads as two players went up for a high cross. He was duly stretchered off and the trainer got to work with the magic sponge. The manager had already used his available substitutes and was desperate to get the player back into the game.

'How is he?' he asked the trainer.

'He's come round,' was the reply, 'but he says he doesn't know who he is.'

'Right,' said the manager. 'Tell him he's Zinedine Zidane and get him back on the park.'

IT IS alleged that Ally McCoist and Bobby Lennox were once having a casual conversation about, funnily enough, football. McCoist asked Lennox how he thought the current Ibrox side, stuffed with expensive foreign players, would make out against the Lisbon Lions (for those who

don't know, Celtic's European Cup-winning side of 1967).
Lennox didn't think it a worthwhile comparison and
refused to say. After some persuasion he finally relented
and suggested that the Lisbon Lions would probably lose
1–0. McCoist was quietly triumphant at this until Lennox
went on to add:

'But you have to remember some of us haven't trained
for twenty-five years.'

A DIEHARD Rangers fan was on holiday with the family
in Florida. One day he left the wife and weans in a queue
at Disney World and went for a wander. He came across
a slightly decrepit shack outside which he read this
roughly-painted sign: 'Wise Old Seminole Chief can answer
any question in the world. Pay one dollar and ask him
whatever you like. If he gets it right you pay him another
25 dollars. If he gets it wrong you win one million dollars!'

The Gers fan is intrigued. Surely he can think up a question that would demand a level of knowledge that some
American Indian can't possibly possess? This sounded like
easy money. He sat down in the shade for a few minutes
until he thought he had a surefire winner. He paid his
dollar admission fee to an elderly Native American woman
at the door of the shack and was told to join the line of
people waiting to talk to the chief, who was sitting cross-
legged on a blanket in a corner of the shack's only room.
As the queue went down, the Gers man congratulated
himself on his ingenuity and was already spending the
money when suddenly it was his turn. The chief looked
at him impassively and nodded slightly to signal him to
put his question.

'Okay,' said the Bluenose, 'who scored the winning goal
in the 1973 Old Firm Cup Final?'

After the briefest of pauses the old chief said:

'Tam Forsyth.'

The Gers fan couldn't believe it: the old guy was right!
How could he possibly know that?

'Next!' grunted the old man, and another eager questioner stepped forward. As the Gers fan was relieved of 25 dollars on his way out he was still struggling to accept what had just happened.

He never forgot the experience and, when the family took another holiday in Florida five years later, he made a point of trying to find out if the old chief was still in business. Sure enough, he was. The old shack was still there, with the same challenge on its sign. The Bluenose was delighted. After all, he had spent hours in the intervening five years concocting a question so obscure and specialised that it was utterly impossible for the chief to know its answer. This time he was onto a definite winner, he congratulated himself as he joined the queue. Wait till the family learned how he had cleverly scored a million bucks! He could hardly contain his joyous anticipation as the people before him took their turn and went away crestfallen as he had five years before. Confronted at last with the old man, who appeared not to have aged in the slightest, he let his high spirits show in his cocky greeting.

'Remember me, chief? How!'

'He knocked it in after a Derek Johnstone header came back off the post. Next!'

AND HERE'S one not about the Old Firm (surprise, surprise!) but a former Glasgow side long since defunct, Third Lanark, once based at Cathkin Park on the Southside. In this age of enormous payments to players and deals negotiated by agents, it is illuminating to consider how things were in an earlier period of the sport.

My father, a former Thirds supporter, told me about meeting a man whom he recognised as a former star centre-forward for his old team before the war. They began to discuss those days and the player gave an insight into how things had been for the club's footballers then, including the fact that the dressing room had no proper hooks but a series of nails banged into the walls.

Apparently, at one time things were so bad that the only boots available for him were of two different sizes. He also told of welcoming a new young player, signed by the club from a YMCA side, and the new signing's disgruntled reaction on learning that, at £2.10s per week, he was earning ten bob less than the older player. The youth, of course, had no agent to enlist to seek redress, so he made as drastic a move as he could. He got his mammy up to see the manager.

IT WAS Wee Billy's birthday. He had been doing very well at school and as a reward, his parents had agreed to take him into town to get him any present he desired. The family were all staunch Rangers supporters and they hadn't the slightest suspicion that their youngest member was harbouring a dark secret. Once in Argyle Street the father sloped off for a quick pint, arranging to meet up later, leaving Wee Billy in the care of his mother and his big brother Robert. It so happened that the trio were passing the Celtic Shop when Billy stopped and seemed fascinated by something in the window.

'Listen, Maw,' he said, 'know how ye said Ah could get anythin Ah wantit?'

'Aye, son, that's right. Just you name it, wee man.'

'Well, see when Dad took us tae the Old Firm game last Saturday? Know who Ah thought wis the best player on the park?'

'Naw. Who?'

'Nakamura!' cried the boy.

At this point, big brother Robert butted in.

'You better be jokin, ya wee rocket.'

'Ah'm no jokin. That Nakamura's pure brilliant, an the present Ah want fur ma birthday is a Celtic shirt wi his name oan it.'

Robert decided that words were not sufficient to express his anger and promptly cuffed his wee brother round the ear. Valiantly restraining tears, determined to fight his corner, Billy insisted that he had been promised anything he wanted, and he was set on getting that shirt.

His outraged mother followed her other son's lead and clouted the boy on the other side of his head.

'Ah'm disgustit!' she told him, 'Ah'm just glad yer Granda's no alive tae see this day or he'd be birlin in his grave.'

She dug out her purse and handed Billy a few banknotes.

'Here, a promise is a promise, but Ah'll no set fit in that shoap. Away in an get it yersel.'

Billy did as he was told and emerged clutching a plastic bag emblazoned in the Celtic colours. His facial expression was rapidly alternating between delight and trepidation as he rejoined his family. His brother took the opportunity of slapping his head again. Just then the father came rolling up.

'Here!' he cried. 'Whit's the idea of hittin yer wee brother, you?'

He listened with growing astonishment as his wife and son explained what had been going on.

'C'mere you!' he growled at Billy before deftly administering a painful kick at the boy's backside. 'Ah canny take it!' he announced, 'Ah'm away back tae the pub.'

Billy's mother grabbed him by the arm and began dragging him along the street, away from the curious onlookers who had begun to gather.

'Ah'd never a thought it,' she complained, 'A boay a mines wi a Celtic shirt! Ah hope you've learned a lesson frae this, boy.' She gave her child a good shake. 'Well, have ye learned a lesson?'

Billy, torn between rubbing his inflamed ears or his bruised bottom, scowled and thought a moment before replying.

'Ah've learned something awright. Ah've only been a Celtic supporter fur ten minutes an Ah hate aw you Huns already.'